Bold 'n' Brassy
Capricorn
ChapStick
MIDOL
Pond's
a lover's concerto
Abraham Martin and John
COTY
Rain drops keep falling on my head
Electric Love penetrates the Sky
Virgo
MILK
pisces
Kleenex
Solid!
we'll sing in the sunshine
Science
Aquarius

YOU LOOK GORGEOUS, RIGHT?

My Perfect Life
HEY MAYBONNE DON'T RIDE ON A BUMMER!
LET'S DO SOMETHING!
Lynda Barry
HarperPerennial

This book is dedicated to Kevin Lavon Kling

 For information address HarperCollins Publishers, Inc., 10 East 53rd Street, New York, NY 10022. FIRST EDITION. ISBN 0-06-096505-3. Edited by Tom Greensfelder and John Mullen! Design by Tom Greensfelder! Kevin Kling on tuba! Julie Wilson on paintbrush! Matt Groening is Funk Lord of USA! Chicago is the best city in the world! But Minneapolis is pretty good too! Go Black-hawks! Go Northstars! Meet me at Lyle's to watch the game!

GO AHEAD, MAYBONNE....
OPEN IT.

BY LYNDA "PRAIRIE FLOWER" BARRY © 1990

THIS YEAR I GOT A CRUDDY DEAL ON ALL MY TEACHERS AND THE MOST SCRUBLY OF LUNCH TIMES: THIRD. BY THIRD LUNCH THE DECENT FOOD'S MOSTLY GONE AND THERE'S SPILLS GALORE ON ALL TABLES, CHAIRS AND THE FLOOR. FOR HOMEROOM I GOT MR. PATZMAN.

FOURTH PERIOD:
MRS. BRISCOE. LANGUAGE ARTS. SHE IS CREATIVE AND WANTS TO COMMUNICATE. SHE WILL FREAK YOU OUT.
HER MOTTO:
"THE ANSWER MY FRIEND, IS BLOWING IN THE WIND."
WHO CAN TELL ME WHY? HANDS?
FIFTH PERIOD:
MATH. MR. NELSON HARDLY TALKS. HARDLY MOVES. HARDLY BREATHES. NICKNAME: MR. NELSON.
HIS MOTTO:
2X + 3Y = 17. 5X = ⁻3 - Y.
X = ? Y = ?
SIXTH PERIOD
P.E. MRS. JARNETT. INTO MAKING YOU FEEL EMBARRASSED. NICKNAME: THE HAIRY EYEBALL
HER MOTTO:
AND NOW A SHOW OF HANDS FROM THOSE WHO HAVE YET TO BEGIN THEIR MENSES?

FOR A LOCKER PARTNER I GOT A GIRL NAMED CORINNA MORTON WHO IS NEW THIS YEAR. SHE HAS SLIGHTLY A HEE-HAW ACCENT AND SHE HAS SAID "YOU ALL" TO ME. I AM TRYING NOT TO BE SHALLOW ABOUT HER DEFECTS BECAUSE I KNOW THE EXPERIENCE OF BEING HARD UP FOR FRIENDS FROM LAST YEAR WHEN I FIRST CAME HERE, BUT I'M TRYING TO FIND SOME ONE TO TRADE PARTNERS WITH. SO FAR NO ONE WILL. SOMETIMES I WONDER: IS THERE A CURSE ON MY LIFE?

HEY MAYBONNE.
UH... HI.
OH GOD
CAN I WALK HOME WITH YOU ALL?
UH...
I GUESS SO.
SAY NO! NO! NO WAY!

DIG ON IT
LYNDA J. BARRY ©1990
DEAR BRENDA, WHAT IS HAPPENING!!! I'M IN HOMEROOM YOU SHOULD SEE THE TEACHER MR. PATZMAN, CALLED "SARGE." A NAME HE MADE UP FOR HIS OWN SELF! CAN YOU IMAGINE DIGGING ON PEOPLE CALLING YOU SARGE? BUT IT FITS HIS PERSONALITY.

FOR SCHOOL CLOTHES THIS YEAR I DIDN'T GET NOTHING THAT GREAT. THE STORES OUT HERE ARE MOSTLY LAME. MOSTLY JUST SEAR'S JR. BAZAAR. I GOT A KIND OF GOOD COUPLE OF DRESSES. SHIRT DRESSES. AND ONE PAIR OF SHOES WITH CHUNKY HEELS BUT THEY KILL MY FEET SO BAD! SARGE IS EXPLAINING HOW THE FLAG IS THE SYMBOL OF OUR FREEDOM.

HE KEEPS TALKING ABOUT FREEDOM BUT HE DOESN'T MEAN THE SAME KIND I AM INTO. IN HIS LIFE IT'S THE FREEDOM TO BOSS PEOPLE AND THE FREEDOM TO MAKE YOU SHUT UP IF YOU GIVE YOUR ARGUEMENT TO HIS OPINION. GUESS WHAT THERE'S A DANCE AFTER SCHOOL. SHOULD I GO? ☐ YES ☐ NO. NEXT PERIOD I GOT MISS FORTNER. HISTORY.

THERE'S SIGN UPS FOR IF YOU WANT TO RUN FOR STUDENT BODY. CINDY LUDERMYER SAYS I SHOULD GO FOR SECRETARY BUT I IT'S LATER NOW I'M IN HISTORY SARGE CAUGHT ME WRITING YOU AND SAID TO READ THE LETTER! I SWEAR TO GOD I ABOUT DID IT JUST TO GIVE HIM SOME REALITY!! LUCKY THING THE BELL RANG. IF YOU COULD SEE MISS FORTNER'S WIG! WHY CAN'T PEOPLE JUST BE ALL THEMSELVES? SORRY! THIS IS MY MOST BORING LETTER BUT SO IS MY LIFE.!!!

WRITE ME! ☮ Maybonne
P.S. KNOCK - KNOCK.

RIIINNG

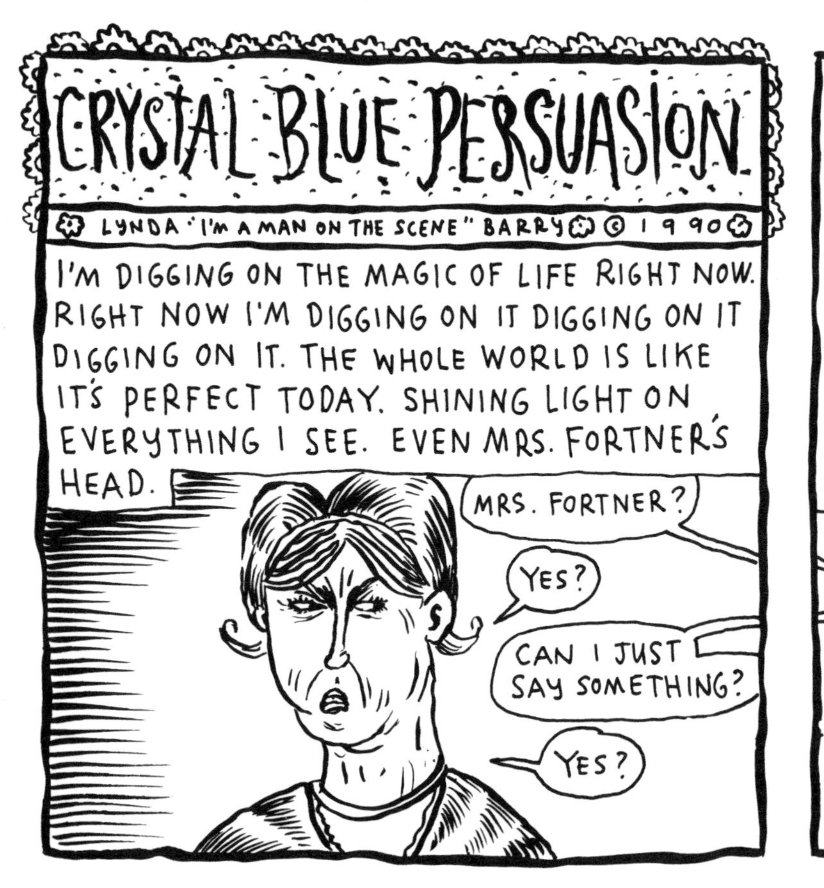
CRYSTAL BLUE PERSUASION
LYNDA "I'M A MAN ON THE SCENE" BARRY © 1990
I'M DIGGING ON THE MAGIC OF LIFE RIGHT NOW. RIGHT NOW I'M DIGGING ON IT DIGGING ON IT DIGGING ON IT. THE WHOLE WORLD IS LIKE IT'S PERFECT TODAY. SHINING LIGHT ON EVERYTHING I SEE. EVEN MRS. FORTNER'S HEAD.
MRS. FORTNER?
YES?
CAN I JUST SAY SOMETHING?
YES?

I BELIEVE IN EVERYONE. I AM HAVING THE RIGHT ON FEELINGS OF LOVE! THERE'S NO REASON! I'M IN A STONED SOUL PICNIC! I'M GRAZING IN THE GRASS! AT LUNCH PEOPLE ARE SAYING MAN I KNOW YOU ARE HIGH! TODAY I AM CRACKING UP AT ALL JOKES! BUT I AM NOT HIGH. EVEN I DON'T GET WHAT'S THIS GOOD MOOD! WHO EVER IS READING THIS, I LOVE YOU. PEACE AND RIGHT ON!
YOU LOOK REALLY NICE RIGHT NOW.

WALKING TO SCHOOL THIS MORNING I WORSHIPPED ALL THINGS. YOU MIGHT SAY THAT'S WARPED! DID I JUST FORGET ABOUT POLLUTION, PREJUDICE AND HOW THERE'S PEOPLE IN A WAR??????????
EXCUSE ME BUT I KNOW THAT! CAN I HELP IT IF RIGHT THIS SECOND I GET SOMETHING INCREDIBLE? I CAN'T HARDLY EXPLAIN IT. EVERYTHING LOOKS LIKE IT'S STARRING IN A MOVIE OF GORGEOUS DETAILS.
DO YOU KNOW WHY YOU'RE HERE?
MRS. FORTNER SEEMS TO BELIEVE YOU'RE ACTING STRANGELY
YOU HAVE A NICE VOICE.

DON'T BARF, BUT I AM SO THANKFUL I GOT BORN. RIGHT ON TO PARAMECIUM! RIGHT ON TO OUTER SPACE! RIGHT ON TO EVOLUTION, REVOLUTION AND THE BALL OF CONFUSION! EXCUSE ME IF I BLOW YOUR MIND, BUT RIGHT ON TO ALL THINGS, 100%, LOVE TRUELY, ☮
Maybonne

SERIOUSLY.

I MEAN IT FOR REAL.

P.S. DEAR GOD PLEASE IF I COULD ONLY JUST REMEMBER THIS FEELING WHEN I AM NEXT DEPRESSED!!!!!

TRUE EXPERIENCE

by L·Y·N·D·A B·A·R·R·Y ©89

AT LUNCH IT GOT ASKED DID YOU EVER HAVE CONTACT WITH A GHOST. PEOPLE KEPT SAYING FOR NANCY NEWBY TO TELL HER STORY AND SHE KEPT GOING "NO."

C'MON NANCE!
LET'S HEAR
NO, YOU GUYS.
NO.
C'MON

THEN SHE WAS MY GYM PARTNER AND ON CURL UPS I ASKED HER, SHE WENT "NO, NO" THEN, "OK. BUT IT'S WEIRD." ONE NIGHT SHE HAD TO PEE, AND THEN SHE SEES A GHOSTLY HAND COMING OUT BY THE TOILET PAPER. SHE SAID DID I BELIEVE HER. THE ANSWER WAS YES.

NOW, NO MATTER WHAT, I HOLD IT.
MAN, I WOULD TOO

YES, BECAUSE NO ONE WOULD LOGICALLY MAKE UP A STORY WITH YOURSELF PEEING IN IT. THEN THE HAND DISAPPEARED. THEN HER BROTHER GARY SAID HE SAW THE SAME HAND! THEY WANTED TO DO AN INVESTIGATION BUT THEIR PARENTS SAID JUST SHUT UP ABOUT IT! IT REMAINS A MYSTERY.

I SAID WE SHOULD DO A SEANCE TO CONTACT THE HAND. WHAT IF IT'S TRYING TO GIVE AN IMPORTANT MESSAGE? WE DID A LEVITATION IN HER BATHROOM. WE ASKED THE HAND TO HELP LIFT CINDY LUDERMYER. WE ONLY USED TWO FINGERS AND SHE WENT STRAIGHT UP! WE SCREAMED AND SHE FELL. THE POWER OF THE HAND IS REAL!

GIRLS! WHAT IS GOING ON IN THERE!!! NANCY! OPEN THIS DOOR!!! NANCY!!!

TO BE CONTINUED!!

THE POWER OF THE HAND IS REAL
BY LYNDA BARRY © 1989
NANCY'S MOTHER WAS PISSED WHEN SHE FOUND OUT ABOUT US CONTACTING THE GHOSTLY HAND IN HER BATHROOM. SHE ASKED US WAS THAT VERY CHRISTIAN. NANCY'S MOTHER IS SO CHRISTIAN NANCY CAN'T EVEN WEAR PANTYHOSE.
SORRY, MOM

SHE TOLD US SATAN IS ALWAYS WATCHING FOR A PLACE TO ENTER OUR HEARTS. IS IT DISRESPECTFUL OF GOD THAT THE WHOLE TIME SHE WAS TALKING I COULDN'T STOP NOTICING SHE WAS WEARING A WIG? CAST THE DEVIL OUT OF YOUR HEARTS. YOU SHOULD BE ASHAMED OF YOURSELVES!! WALKING HOME, WE ALL FELT CRUDDY.

AT SCHOOL I TOLD NANCY SORRY FOR GETTING HER IN TROUBLE. SHE SAID SHE WAS USED TO IT. THEN BY MY LOCKER IT WAS HER WHO BROUGHT UP THE HAND. SHE SAID WOULD I DO A SEANCE WITH HER IN THE GIRL'S CAN TO TRY AND MOVE THE GHOSTLY HAND OUT OF HER BATHROOM TO THE SCHOOL BATHROOM. NANCY'S MY FRIEND I HAD TO SAY YES.

WE WENT INTO STALL # 5. IN A WAY I WAS SERIOUSLY FREAKED OUT. OH HAND PLEASE LEAVE THE BATHROOM OF 3212 S. GRANDON AND COME TO THE LAVATORY OF SELMER JR. HIGH. OH HAND. THEN THIS GIRL SUE ACKER YANKS OPEN THE STALL. SHE SAW US HOLDING HANDS SO NOW THE WHOLE SCHOOL THINKS WE'RE LESBOS. IF THE POWER OF THE HAND IS REAL PLEASE CHOKE SUE ACKER.

SPILL the WINE

LYNDA BARRY ©1989

SUE ACKER IS SUCH A BITCH. I TOLD HER WHY I WAS HOLDING HANDS WITH NANCY NEWBY IN THE CAN. I TOLD HER IT WAS A SEANCE TO CONTACT THE GHOSTLY HAND. BUT SHE PASSES IT AROUND THAT NANCY AND ME ARE LESBIAN QUEERS TOGETHER. OH GREAT.

AND I KNOW WHY TOO. BECAUSE I SAID THIS THING ONE TIME ABOUT WHAT'S WRONG WITH QUEERS? BECAUSE SUE ACKER (THE BITCH!) (I'M GOING TO WRITE BITCH EVERY TIME AFTER HER NAME BECAUSE SHE IS A BITCH. A BITCH TO THE 10TH POWER!) BECAUSE SHE IS ALWAYS SAYING EVERYONE'S A QUEER. I SAID I LIKED THAT SONG **LOLA** AND SHE SAID IT'S A QUEER'S SONG ABOUT QUEERS. ALSO THAT THE GUY WHO SANG SPILL THE WINE'S A QUEER.

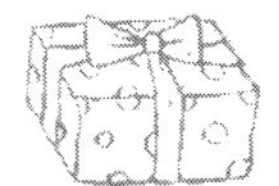

HER WHOLE LIFE IS WHO'S A QUEER AND NOW I'M A QUEER BECAUSE I DON'T THINK QUEERS ARE WEIRD BUT I WAS EVEN STUPID TO SAY IT BECAUSE I FORGOT THIS IS A PLASTIC WORLD SO IF YOU HAVE A FREE MIND, BETTER SHUT UP. ALSO HOW COULD THE SPILL THE WINE GUY BE QUEER IF HE'S SINGING TO A GIRL? SUE ACKER (THE BITCH[10]) SAYS HE'S HIDING IT BUT YOU CAN ALWAYS TELL.

THEN I NOTICE NANCY NEWBY WON'T HAVE NOTHING TO DO WITH ME AND ALSO SOME **OTHER GIRLS.** AT LUNCH NO ONE TALKED TO ME AT THE TABLE THAT MUCH AND EVERYONE KEPT LOOKING AT EACH OTHER. THEN THERE'S THE WORD LESBO ON MY LOCKER IN GREEN EL MARKO. I GO "NANCY TELL THE TRUTH OF WHAT HAPPENED SO I CAN HAVE PROOF" AND NANCY JUST KEEPS WALKING.

WHAT IS BETTER?

LYNDA · BARRY © 1989

I AM NOT A LESBIAN. SUE ACKER IS TELLING THE UNIVERSE I AM BUT I'M NOT. TODAY SHE TOLD AT LUNCH HOW I DON'T THINK QUEERS ARE SICK. I SAID QUEERS ARE EQUAL TO ANYBODY BECAUSE THAT'S MY TRUE OPINION, OK?

BUT IN HER BRAIN IT EQUALS: THEN I EQUAL A LESBIAN, WHICH ALSO EQUALS: THAT NO GIRLS WILL TALK TO ME AND THE BOYS SHOUT LESBO. I DON'T EVEN GET HOW THIS HAPPENED. THEN THIS ONE GUY DOUG SAYS "WANT TO PROVE YOU'RE NOT?" THEN HE SAYS THINGS ABOUT BALLING.

HE PUT HIS ARM AROUND ME AFTER 6TH PERIOD I JUST LET HIM SO SUE ACKER WOULD SEE. IN A WAY RIGHT NOW A BOYFRIEND WOULD SOLVE EVERYTHING. DOUG LIVES BY THE POWER LINES IN THE DEVELOPMENT. IS IT BETTER TO BE A LESBIAN OR A SLUT?

HE PUT HIS HAND UNDER MY SHIRT IF YOU COULD HEAR THE POWERLINES HOW THEY MAKE A NOISE LIKE YOUR BRAIN IS ON NO CHANNEL YOU JUST CLOSE YOUR EYES AND SEE THE TV PICTURE OF THOSE MILLION DOTS JUMPING. I GET HOME AND MY GRANDMA YELLS I'M LATE. TOMORROW HE'LL TELL THEM AND I PROMISE I WILL SHUT UP ABOUT QUEERS. I PROMISE.

THINGS CAN CHANGE
L·Y·N·D·A B·A·R·R·Y ©1989
YOU KNOW HOW YOUR LIFE IS JUST SUPPOSED TO BE GETTING BETTER AND BETTER, RIGHT? LIKE IN THE MOVIES WHERE IT GETS TERRIBLE BUT THEN THE END IS SUDDENLY MAGICAL? BUT WHAT IF YOUR LIFE KEEPS GOING ON BAD?
DOUG
DOUG
HEY DOUG,

IN OLD YELLER THE SADDEST PART FOR THE BOY IS WHEN OLD YELLER GETS RABIES AND THE BOY HAS TO SHOOT HIM. THEN THE END GETS SUDDENLY MAGICAL FOR THE BOY, BECAUSE HE GETS ONE OF OLD YELLER'S PUPPIES. BUT FOR OLD YELLER THERE IS NO SUDDENLY MAGICAL PART. HE LOOKS AT THE BOY AND THE BOY SHOOTS HIM.
WHAT.
UH...
NOTHING.
HI.

FOR THINGS TO GET SUDDENLY MAGICAL YOU HAVE TO BE THE STAR. I LOOK AT THE PEOPLE AT MY SCHOOL. I SAY, IF THIS WAS A MOVIE, WHO WOULD BE THE STAR? IF A GUY FEELS YOU UP AND YOU KNOW HE'S JUST USING YOU AND YOU LET HIM, THAT EQUALS A SLUT. A SLUT CAN'T BE THE STAR, SO IT'S NOT ME.

ARE YOU THAT HARD UP, MYERS?

SHUT UP PATRICELLI!

BOW WOW!

SHUT UP

DOUG?

DOUG.

THE "SUDDENLY MAGICAL" ISN'T GOING TO HAPPEN TO ME. EXCEPT ONE WAY ONLY: IF DOUG WILL BE IN LOVE WITH ME. IF DOUG FEELS ME UP BUT IS IN LOVE, I DON'T COUNT AS A SLUT. WHAT A PERFECT ENDING. IF ONLY I CAN MAKE HIM LOVE ME. IF ONLY I CAN BE JUST PERFECT FOR HIM IT WOULD BE SUCH A BEAUTIFUL ENDING.

WHAT?!
NOTHING.
WANNA GO FOR ANOTHER WALK AGAIN?

FOR ONE THING THE SONG IS BEAUTIFUL AND I THINK YOU ARE A BEAUTIFUL PERSON. EVEN THOUGH YOU DON'T TALK TO ME ANY MORE EVER SINCE OUR THING AT THE PARK I KNOW YOU WEREN'T JUST USING ME. PEOPLE CAN BE SO COLD BLOODED, THE THINGS THEY SAY TO TRY TO BRING EACH OTHER DOWN. SOME GIRLS WHOSE NAMES I WON'T TELL TRIED TO BRING ME DOWN AT LUNCH BY SAYING YOU SAID SOME THINGS ABOUT ME LIKE HOW FLAT I AM.

HEY

"I THINK YOU ARE A BEAUTIFUL PERSON"

GIVE IT

ALSO THAT WE BALLED. I JUST LAUGHED IN THEIR FACES AND THEN I JUST KEPT ON TRUCKIN' BECAUSE FROM KNOWING YOU LIKE I DO IT'S SO OBVIOUSLY A LIE THAT YOU WOULD EVER SAY ANYTHING LIKE THAT. ANOTHER PART OF THE SONG GOES: I LOVE YOU FOR WHO YOU ARE NOT THE ONE YOU FEEL YOU NEED TO BE. I HOPE THAT DOESN'T MAKE YOU FEEL WEIRD BUT IT'S TRUE.

HEY MAN. YOU SAID YOU DID IT WITH HER.
YEAH. I DID.
SHE SAYS YOU'RE LYIN'
YEAH. SURE.

IT'S NOT LIKE I'M SAYING I WANT YOU FOR MY BOYFRIEND. BECAUSE I WANT YOU TO BE FREE. JUST THAT YOU'VE GOT A FRIEND. MY PHONE NUMBER IS PA5-4456. IF YOU EVER FEEL DOWN AND NO ONE CAN UNDERSTAND YOU I ALWAYS WILL. I HOPE YOU DON'T THINK THIS LETTER IS STUPID. EVEN IF YOU NEVER SPEAK TO ME AGAIN I'LL NEVER SAY YOU'RE A USER BECAUSE YOU'RE NOT. PEACE. LOVE MAYBONNE

P.S. I AM NOT SAYING I DON'T WANT TO BE YOUR GIRLFRIEND! THAT'S THE MOST BEAUTIFUL THING I CAN IMAGINE!

PERFECT

BY LYNDA BARRY © 1990

THE NEW THING AT MY SCHOOL IS FOR YOU TO BE YOURSELF. I DON'T GET WHAT THAT IS EVEN SUPPOSED TO MEAN. IT'S OK ADVICE IF YOURSELF IS BEAUTIFUL BUT WHAT DO YOU DO INCASE YOURSELF REALLY SUCKS?

DO YOU JUST DO A THING OF JUST KEEP ON SAYING: IN REALITY I AM BEAUTIFUL? THEN WHAT IF YOU TURN CONCEITED? ALSO I DON'T GET IT IF YOU LIKE A GUY AND YOU BE YOURSELF, AND HE STILL DOESN'T LIKE YOU. ARE YOU JUST SUPPOSED TO SAY THAT'S BEAUTIFUL ALSO?

LIKE FOR EXAMPLE DOUG. I SHOWED HIM MY FEELINGS AND NOW I AM INVISIBLE TO HIM. WHAT I DON'T GET IS HOW CAN A GUY FRENCH YOU AND THEN LATER YOU DON'T EVEN EXIST? I AM TRYING TO DO THAT IDEA OF THE POEM "YOU ARE A CHILD OF THE UNIVERSE," BUT SOMETIMES IT IS SO HARD.

OH DOUG. THE TRAGEDY OF LIFE IS HOW PERFECT YOU ARE FOR ME. I ALWAYS THOUGHT IT BEFORE, BUT WHEN YOU QUIT LIKING ME, I KNEW IT FOR SURE.

MY ASSIGNMENT

by Lynda Barry © 1990

THERE IS AN IDEA THAT BAD THINGS IN LIFE ARE ACTUALLY BEAUTIFUL BECAUSE EVEN THE MOST BUMMER OF AN EXPERIENCE CAN GIVE YOU DEVELOPMENT. THAT WAS OUR ASSIGNMENT TODAY IN LANGUAGE ARTS. WRITE A POEM ON THE CONCEPT OF THIS CONCEPT.

OF COURSE MY TOPIC WAS THE BUMMER OF DOUG. UNTIL HIM, I BELIEVED IN THE GREATNESS OF: ALL YOU NEED IS LOVE. UNTIL HIM, I NEVER PERSONALLY KNEW THAT SOMEONE COULD LIE AND USE YOU, THEN BE SO FREEZING COLD TO **ALL** THE SADNESS OF YOUR FEELINGS. ALSO, UNTIL HIM I DIDN'T KNOW I COULD BE SUCH A STUPID IDIOT.

NOW THAT I KNOW THESE THINGS, AM I REALLY SUPPOSED TO SAY THANK YOU? AM I SHALLOW TO MAKE THE BACKWARDS WISH OF: DO OVERS? STAR LIGHT, STAR BRIGHT. GOD, IS IT INSULTING TO YOU THAT I WONDER WHY YOU LET ALL THE SUFFERING POUR DOWN? IS IT SO PEOPLE WILL TRY TO FIND YOU? ARE YOU REALLY THAT BIG AND WORTH IT?

MY POEM WAS CALLED "I CAN'T FAKE IT" WHERE I SAID SOMETIMES BAD THINGS ARE **TRULY** BAD AND THAT THE ONLY GOOD PART ABOUT MY THING WITH DOUG IS THAT IT'S OVER.
MISS HOLLIS GAVE ME A C-, AND WROTE ON THE TOP OF MY PAPER "DIDN'T YOU UNDERSTAND THE ASSIGNMENT?"

I GOT BETTER

by LYNDA BARRY ©1990

FOR AROUND 27 DAYS AFTER DOUG QUIT LIKING ME, MY LIFE WAS PURE BARF. I THOUGHT I'M GOING TO KILL MYSELF. HOW COULD LIFE BE WORTH IT WITHOUT DOUG EVEN IF HE DID USE ME? BUT THEN IT TURNED OUT I WAS TOO CHICKEN.

EVEN WHEN I GOT TIRED OF THINKING OF HIM I STILL KEPT THINKING OF HIM. I KEPT HAVING BRAIN ATTACKS OF HIS FACE IN MY MIND. AND I COULD NOT EAT BECAUSE ALL FOOD WAS BARF TO ME ALSO. I WAS JUST THANKFUL FOR WINSTONS, L+Ms, SALEMS, PALL MALLS, VICEROYS, LARKS, AND OLD GOLDS.

ALL MY FRIENDS GAVE ME THEIR DIF-FERENT PHILOSOPHYS OF WHAT A CRUD HE IS AND HOW HE NEVER EVEN LIKED ME FOR REAL, HE WAS JUST PLAYING ME FOR CHEAP. AND IT WAS TRUE THAT IN SOME WAYS HE DID DO ME COLD BLOODED AND HE BURNED ME BUT I ALWAYS KNEW HOW HE WAS BEAUTIFUL INSIDE.

THEN FINALLY I NOTICED I WAS NOT THINKING OF HIM SO BEAUTIFULLY. THEN I WAS HARDLY THINKING OF HIM AT ALL AND I WAS STARTING TO LIKE THIS OTHER GUY, BOB AND THAT'S WHEN MY MIRACLE HAPPENED. JUST IN TIME. DOUG CALLED ME AGAIN. LIFE CAN BE SO MAGICAL.

THE CHANGES

BY LYNDA BARRY ©1990

PEOPLE SAY YOU CAN CHANGE YOURSELF. FOR EXAMPLE IF YOU HAVE A DEFECTIVE PERSONALITY YOU CAN KEEP ON STRIVING AND SOON YOU WILL WALK IN THE RAYS OF A BEAUTIFUL SUN.

BUT IF A GUY YOU LIKE IS DEFECTIVE AND DOES THINGS COLD BLOODED TO YOU, PEOPLE SAY CLOSE THE DOOR BECAUSE NO WAY IS HE EVER GOING TO CHANGE. PERSONALLY I DON'T GET THE DIFFERENCE.

DOUG SAYS NOW HE WANTS TO BE MY BOYFRIEND BUT DON'T TELL ANYONE BECAUSE IT'S TOO COMPLICATED. I TOLD ONE PERSON, NANCY NEWBY AND SHE SAID SEE HOW HE'S USING YOU BEFORE IT'S TOO LATE BUT DOUG, I BELIEVE IN YOU AND TRUST IS OUR MOST BEAUTIFUL THING. NOTHING CAN DESTROY IT.

HOW COME YOU KEEP STANDIN' BY THE PHONE?
SHUT UP!

SO WHAT IF YOU DIDN'T CALL ME TONIGHT AND SO WHAT IF YOU WENT TO THE GAME WITH CINDY LUDERMYER? I KNOW IT'S LIKE YOU SAID. YOU HAVE TO EXPRESS YOURSELF AND YOU DON'T WANT NO ONE TO BE A CHAIN ON YOU. AND I KNOW WHAT WE HAVE IS SECRETLY BEAUTIFUL BECAUSE BEAUTIFUL GOD LET YOU COME BACK TO ME. I PRAYED AND HE LET YOU COME BACK. THANK YOU SO MUCH.

WHAT'S YOUR PROBLEM?

I SAID SHUT UP!!!

NO QUIET
BY WILLIAM SHAKESPEARE SONNET NO. 27 · Pictures by L. Barry © 90
WEARY WITH TOIL I HASTE ME TO MY BED THE DEAR REPOSE FOR LIMBS WITH TRAVEL TIRED; BUT THEN BEGINS A JOURNEY IN MY HEAD
TO WORK MY MIND WHEN BODY'S WORK EXPIRED. FOR THEN MY THOUGHTS,

FAR FROM WHERE I ABIDE, INTEND A ZEALOUS PILGRIMAGE TO THEE. AND KEEP MY DROOPING EYELIDS OPEN WIDE LOOKING ON DARKNESS WHICH THE BLIND DO SEE; SAVE THAT MY SOUL'S IMAGINARY SIGHT PRESENTS THY SHADOW TO MY SIGHTLESS VIEW,

OH DOUG

WHICH, LIKE A JEWEL HUNG IN GHASTLY NIGHT MAKES BLACK NIGHT BEAUTEOUS AND HER OLD FACE NEW. LO, THUS, BY DAY MY LIMBS, BY NIGHT MY MIND,

FOR THEE, AND FOR MYSELF NO QUIET FIND.
MAYBONNE!!
HUH? WHAT?
THIS IS THE LAST TIME I'M WARNING YOU ABOUT SLEEPING IN CLASS!

My Question

LYNDA BARRY 1990

DEAR GOD. NO OFFENSE, BUT I AM WONDERING ABOUT YOU. I HEARD YOU WORK IN MYSTERIOUS WAYS BUT NOW YOU ARE BLOWING MY MIND OUT. FOR EXAMPLE, HOW I PRAYED TO YOU TO GET DOUG BACK FOR ME.

I MEAN THANK YOU AND ALL BUT THIS THING WHERE HE SAYS I CAN'T TELL ANYBODY THAT HE'S MY BOYFRIEND, I THINK SORT OF SUCKS. I'M NOT TRYING TO DO A CRITICISM OF YOU BUT REMEMBER I ASKED FOR BEAUTIFUL LOVE WITH HIM? IF THIS IS BEAUTIFUL PLEASE SHOW ME HOW. I NEED SOME HINTS BAD.

THE KISSES PART I WILL ADMIT THAT'S BEAUTIFUL. TRUELY I LOVE HIS GORGEOUS KISSES BUT THE OTHER PARTS. IS IT A SIN? ALSO HIS THING WITH CINDY LUDERMYER. HE SAYS THEY ARE JUST FRIENDS BUT AT THE GAME PEOPLE SAID THEY WERE HOLDING HANDS. MY QUESTION IS WHAT ARE YOU GOING TO DO IF CINDY LUDERMYER PRAYS FOR DOUG ALSO? IS SHE MORE EQUAL THAN ME? DOES IT COUNT THAT I PRAYED FIRST?

OUR FATHER WHO ART IN HEAVEN, DID YOU NOTICE THE RED CANDLE I LIT FOR YOU AT ST. ANTHONYS? NO BRAG, BUT I DID PUT $2.75 IN THAT BOX. MY LIFE FEELS SO MESSED UP. IN THE NAME OF THE FATHER, SON, AND HOLY GHOST IF IT TURNS OUT DOUG IS JUST USING ME I WILL DIE.

THE CONCEPT OF DOUG
BY LYNDA BARRY © 1990
WHAT I DON'T GET IS: WHY IS THERE WAR, WHY IS THERE POLLUTION, WHY IS THERE STARVATION AND WHY DO GUYS QUIT LIKING YOU WHEN YOU START LIKING THEM?
GIRLS

THAT WAS THE MAIN CONCEPT OF DOUG. HE DROPPED ME THEN HE SAID COME BACK. WHEN I WENT BACK, HE QUIT ME AGAIN. NOW CINDY LUDERMYER LOVES HIM. WHEN SHE DIDN'T, HE WENT AFTER HER. NOW SHE IS CRYING IN THE GIRL'S BATHROOM EVERY DAY.

I KNOW HER FEELING OF LOVING DOUG. WHEN I FIRST WENT IN THE GIRL'S CAN AND SAW HER SO MESSED UP, I ABOUT DID A BARF RIGHT ON THE FLOOR FROM MY RELATING. IT WAS LIKE SMELLING THE SMELL OF A FOOD YOU THREW UP ON. I USED TO HAVE IT ABOUT HORMEL BEEF STEW. NOW I HAVE IT ABOUT DOUG.

I TRIED TO TELL CINDY THE CONCEPT OF DOUG, BUT SHE JUST THOUGHT I WAS TRYING TO POISON HER MIND AGAINST HIM. I GUESS LOVE IS A DEAL WHERE YOU HAVE TO LEARN YOUR OWN EVIDENCE BECAUSE WHEN I TOLD HER "SOMEDAY YOU WILL BE FREE" SHE JUST TURNED AROUND AND GAVE ME THE DELUXE FINGER.

PRETTY MUCH SO FAR EVERYONE IS SAYING YES. YOU CAN GROOVE ON FORGIVENESS AND UNDERSTANDING AND THE ANSWER IS YES. THEN I GO "BUT SECRETLY?" BUT SECRETLY IN YOUR MOST SECRETEST MIND ACTIONS CAN YOU EVER TRUST SOMEONE WHO DOGGED YOU BAD?

I AM BEING SO FOR REAL AND YOU ARE BEING SO COLD.

LIKE BEEFARONI THAT YOU BARFED ON WON'T YOU ALWAYS KIND OF RE-MEMBER IT EVEN WHEN YOU TRY TO FORGET? AS SOON AS THE CAN OPENER GOES IN THE CAN AND THE MOST MIDGET SMELL OF IT COMES UP I REMEMBER I REMEMBER I REMEMBER.

I TOLD YOU SO MANY TIMES I'M SORRY.

COME ON MAN.

DOUG SAYS MY PROBLEM IS THAT HE HAS CHANGED BUT I WILL NOT HAVE A FREE MIND ABOUT THIS AND GIVE HIM ANOTHER CHANCE. IF ON THE LABEL IT SAYS PEACHES AND YOU OPEN IT AND SEE BEEFARONI WHAT SHOULD YOU DO? HE KEEPS CALLING ME AND I AM STARTING TO MISS HIM.

THE MOST OBVIOUS QUESTION
LYNDA BARRY
©1992

IT WAS COMING TO BE CHRISTMAS VACATION. I GOT THE IDEA TO TAKE THE GREYHOUND BUS BACK TO SEE MOM.
WHY THE HELL YOU WANT TO SEE HER FOR? SHE NEVER DID YOU NO FAVORS.
I JUST WANT TO.
YOU THINK SHE WANTS TO SEE YOU?

ME AND MY SISTER HAD BEEN LIVING AT MY GRANDMA'S OVER ONE YEAR. IT STARTED AS A VACATION.
THAT WOMAN'S SO DAMN HIGH STRUNG.
I TRIED TO TELL YOUR FATHER WHEN HE MARRIED HER
DID HE LISTEN TO ME?

WHEN TIME CAME TO GO HOME, INSTEAD YOU SAW US STANDING IN THE SEAR'S STORE, MY GRANDMA WITH HER CHARGE CARD OUT AND US BUYING SCHOOL CLOTHES.
HELL NO. HE JUST RUN OFF AND MARRY HER AND THE NEXT THING I KNOW SHE'S POOPING OUT TWO KIDS.
NOW LOOK WHO'S GOT 'EM.

WHY DIDN'T WE GO BACK? SOME-TIMES THE MOST OBVIOUS QUESTION IS THE ONE YOU'LL NEVER ASK.
THEM TWO DESERVED EACH OTHER.
BUT THEY NEVER HAD NO BUSINESS HAVING KIDS.

"WELL," MY GRANDMA SAID, "SHE'S YOUR MOTHER. IF YOU WANT TO GO SEE HER I CAN'T STOP YOU."
CHRIST. I GIVE UP.
BUT YOU TALK TO HER. I'VE HAD MY FILL OF THAT WOMAN.

THE DEAL WAS I HAD TO CALL MOM AND TELL HER I WAS COMING. I GOT ALONE WITH THE TELEPHONE BUT I JUST COULDN'T DIAL IT. IF SHE ANSWERED WHAT WOULD I SAY?

WHEN I CAME BACK INTO THE KITCHEN MY GRANDMA SAID "WELL?" AND I SAID "SHE'S HAPPY. SHE'S HAPPY I'M COMING."
AND WHAT DID SHE HAVE TO SAY ABOUT YOU TAKING THE BUS HALFWAY ACROSS THE COUNTRY BY YOURSELF?
NOTHING.
SHE THINKS I'M OLD ENOUGH.

I FIGURED I'D CALL HER LATER BUT THEN IT WAS THE NIGHT BEFORE I LEFT AND I STILL HADN'T DONE IT. I WAS LAYING IN THE DARK AND PICTURES WERE COMING TO ME LIKE DREAMS.

ONE THOUSAND PICTURES FLYING LIKE THE PROJECTOR WAS TURNED ON MY EYES AND WOULDN'T QUIT RUNNING.

I SAW THEM. HIM DRIVING AND HER TOUCHING HIS BACK. SHE'S HOLDING MY SISTER AND I'M WATCHING. JUST WATCHING.

THEN A SOCK IN THE STOMACH. MY SISTER. IT WAS MORNING. "I HATE YOU!" SHE SAID. "I'M COMING WITH YOU! MOM WANTS TO SEE ME!"
QUIT!
KNOCK IT OFF!
I'M GOIN'!
I AM!

WE WERE ALMOST LATE FOR THE BUS. GRANDMA HANDING ME A BAG OF FOOD AND TEN DOLLARS TO THE BUS MAN TO KEEP AN EYE ON ME.
OH DON'T YOU WORRY MA'AM
AND YOU CALL ME WHEN YOU GET THERE UNDERSTAND?
LET ME GO!!

I TOOK A SEAT IN THE MIDDLE AND THEN I MOVED TO THE BACK. I LOOK OUT THE WINDOW AT THE WORLD FROZEN SOLID.

WHEN THE BUS STARTED MOVING I WATCHED GRANDMA PUSHING MARLYS BACK TO THE CAR. I'LL CALL HER AT THE FIRST STOP. AT THE FIRST STOP I WILL CALL HER AND SAY "SURPRISE!"

"SURPRISE, MOM. IT'S ME."

AT LACROSSE THE DRIVER GOT OFF AND ANOTHER DRIVER GOT ON. BEHIND HIM CAME TONY. AN 18 YEAR OLD SOLDIER FROM WALLACE IDAHO. IS IT GOD WHO MAKES THINGS HAPPEN?
ANYONE SITTIN' HERE?

AND WHY DID I EVEN DO IT? I TOLD HIM MY NAME WAS PAM AND I GAVE HIM LIED DETAILS ABOUT MY LIFE. CAN I HELP IT IF HE BELIEVED EVERYTHING?

IN THE PITCH BLACK NIGHT WITH THE LIGHTS OF THE HIGHWAY SLIDING OVER US HE WAS FRENCHING ME.

BETWEEN MOOREHEAD AND FARGO WITH THE UNIVERSE DEAD ASLEEP HE FELT ME UP.

DEAR MOM HOW ARE YOU I AM IN NORTH DAKOTA IT IS SNOWING AND HIS HANDS ARE PULLING MY SHIRT UP.

I COULD SEE POLES FLOATING BY. THE SKY WAS GETTING LIGHTER. JUMPING BLACK WIRES AND THE RUNNING LINE OF THE SHAPING EARTH.

IN DICKENSON THE DRIVER SAYS "45 MINUTES, FOLKS" I CLIMB PAST TONY. TONY WITH HIS EYES SHUT AND HIS MOUTH WIDE OPEN AND BREATH THAT IS SERIOUSLY BLOWING MY MIND.

SHE'S GETTING READY FOR WORK RIGHT NOW. THE RADIO ON HER STATION AND THE COFFEE POT GOING. I GUESS HER LIFE IS PROBABLY A LOT EASIER.

BY THE PHONE BOOTH I SEE A WOMAN FROM THE BUS TALKING TO THE DRIVER AND POINTING AT ME. I BUY POTATO CHIPS AND MILK AND THEN HE'S COMING OVER.
EXIT
TELEPHO

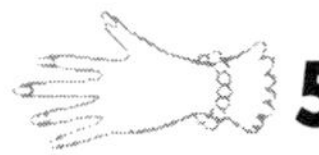

HE TELLS ME THE GREYHOUND POLICY OF SAFE TRAVEL FOR ALL PASSENGERS AND THAT MY NEW SEAT IS BY HIM. IN FRONT BY HIM AND THE WOMAN.

THEY'RE MAKIN' ME MOVE.
HUH?
THEY'RE MAKIN' ME MOVE.

"I GOT A NIECE ABOUT YOUR AGE." THE LADY HANDS ME A PICTURE OF A GIRL WITH A LAME HAIRCUT. THE WHOLE TIME SHE'S TALKING I JUST STARE OUT THE WINDOW.

YOU'RE MAD AT ME NOW BUT SOMEONE AT THE OTHER END IS GONNA BE THANKING ME BY GOD.

SHE DOESN'T KNOW ANYTHING SO WHY DOESN'T SHE JUST SHUT-UP?

ON MY WAY TO THE CAN I LEAN BY TONY AND HE SAYS SOME WORDS TO ME. THEN MY NAME ON THE BUS SPEAKER. NOT MY REAL NAME. THE DRIVER SAYING "PAM."

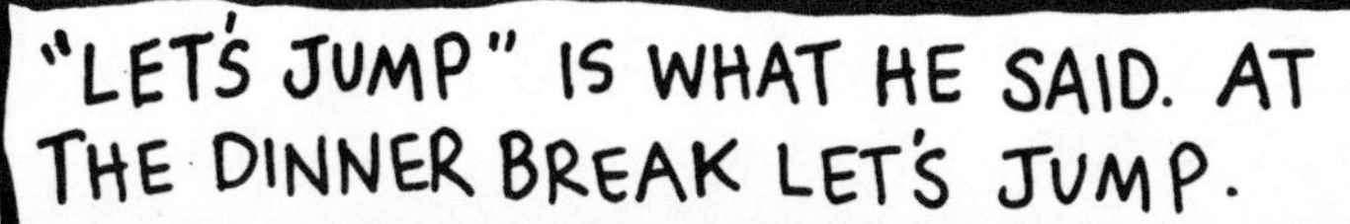

"LET'S JUMP" IS WHAT HE SAID. AT THE DINNER BREAK LET'S JUMP.

TONY PASSES ME IN THE LINE OF PEOPLE GETTING OFF. THE LADY IS ASLEEP AND THE BUS DRIVER IS TALKING TO SOMEONE ELSE.

AROUND THE CORNER FROM THE STATION WALKS TONY AND I FOLLOW TRYING NOT TO RUN.

"LET'S GO!" HE GRABS MY ARM AND WE'RE TEARING DOWN THE BLACK STREET. TONY AND PAM. THE PERFECT COUPLE.

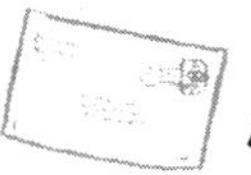

BY A LIT STORE WINDOW WE STOP. SANTA MOVING HIS ARM UP AND DOWN AND A MIDGET TRAIN RUNNING AROUND HIS LEGS. A KEY SHOP. THE MAN LOOKS AT US AND WE KEEP WALKING.

RAILROAD TRACKS. CHRISTMAS LIGHTS ON CRUDDY HOUSES GETTING CRUDDIER. JUMPING LIGHTS OF T.V.S. NO ONE KNOWS WHERE I AM.
WE MISS THE BUS AND THEY JUST STICK US ON THE NEXT ONE.
YOUR STUFF'S OK. THEY STICK IT ON A SHELF IN A ROOM.
HOW MUCH MONEY YOU GOT?

"I DON'T KNOW" I SAY. "COME ON PAM," HE SAYS. "DON'T YOU WANT US TO BE TOGETHER?" I STOP. "MY MOM." I SAY. "SCREW HER." HE SAYS. "SHE DITCHED YOU." THE ONE TRUTH I TOLD HIM.

FREEZING HANDS ON MY FACE. MY NEW IDENTITY SAYS OK. YEAH OK. MERRY CHRISTMAS MOM.

HE KISSES ME. "YOU'RE A SEXY LITTLE MAMA." BY A BAR HE TELLS ME WAIT ACROSS THE STREET BUT FIRST GIVE HIM FIVE DOLLARS.
NEW PARIS
1626
NO MINORS
Miller HIGH LIFE

I WATCH HIM GO IN THE BAR. RIGHT NOW I COULD RUN FOR IT. I COULD. I COULD RUN RIGHT NOW.

ONE BOTTLE OF WINE. "CHUG A LUG CHUG A LUG" TONY SINGS "MAKES YOU WANNA HOLLER HI-DEE-HO"

TONY TRIES THE DOOR HANDLES OF CARS. ONE OPENS. HIM AND THE SEXY LITTLE MAMA GET IN. HE HOLDS THE BOTTLE TO HER MOUTH LIKE A BABY.

THE FEELING IS FLOATING, FLOATING IN THE FROZEN AIR WITH HER PANTS PULLED DOWN AND THE WARM HARD OF TONY TRYING TO PUSH. CHUG A LUG CHUG A LUG.

THE CAR DOOR OPENS AND HER HEAD FALLS BACK. SHE SEES THE BARE NAKED STREET. A POLICEMAN'S FEET STANDING.

HE PULLS HER OUT ONE WAY AND TONY GOES THE OTHER. TONY'S HANDS GRAB HER THEN PEEL OFF. RED LIGHTS FLASHING. HER PANTS YANK UP. PAM BARFS.

THIS IS THE STORY OF PAM, NOT ME. I WAS BORN TWO DAYS AFTER CHRISTMAS. A NOTHING DAY WHEN PEOPLE ARE SICK OF PRESENTS. OH HOLY NIGHT THE STARS ARE BRIGHTLY SHINING.
POLICE

THE BEST PART IS THEY NEVER HANDED ME THE PHONE WHEN THEY CALLED MOM. I GUESS SHE JUST DIDN'T ASK TO TALK TO ME.

THE NEXT BUS WAS TOMORROW. THEY TOOK ME TO A LADY'S HOUSE. CAROLYN. SHE CAME TO THE DOOR IN A ROBE.

I SAT ON HER COUCH. ON HER TREE IT WAS ALL BLUE LIGHTS. I WAS BACK IN MY PERSONAL IDENTITY. I COULD TELL BY MY HORRIBLE FEELINGS.

SHE HANDS ME A TOWEL FOR THE SHOWER AND SAYS IF I GOT PENETRATED TO TELL HER NOW. "NO." I SAY. SHE STARES AT ME. "I DIDN'T." SHE POINTS ME TO THE BATHROOM.

IN THE KITCHEN SHE TELLS ME SHE'S SEEN A LOT OF GIRLS LIKE ME. SHE DRAWS THE MAP OF WHERE I WILL END UP WITH HER FINGERS ON THE TABLE.

SHE HAS A DOG, BOOTSIE. "CAN I HOLD HIM?" I SAY. THE SMELL OF A DOG HAS ALWAYS MADE ME FEEL BETTER.

CAROLYN GIVES ME A CHRISTIAN INSTRUCTION BOOK THAT HAS A GIRL ON THE COVER WITH A MESSED UP EXPRES-SION. IT'S TIME TO SLEEP. "PRAY AND GO TO SLEEP" SHE SAYS.

IN THE MORNING THE POLICEMAN HOLDS THE SCREEN DOOR OPEN. IN THE CAR HE TELLS ME WHAT HE WOULD DO TO ME IF I WAS HIS KID.

AT A STOPLIGHT I SEE THE STORE WITH THE SANTA. HIS ARM FROZEN STILL. I DON'T NOTICE THE REST OF THE WAY TO THE STATION.
KE
MA

FINALLY COMES THE BUS. THE POLICEMAN TALKS TO THE DRIVER. DON'T WORRY ABOUT IT MISTER. I'M MY TRUE SELF NOW. TOO CHICKEN TO DO ANYTHING.

YOU HAVE TO UNDERSTAND. IT WOULD BE EASY IF SHE WOULD JUST SCREAM AT ME OR HIT ME BUT THAT'S NOT HER WAY. SHE JUST STARES.

BARFING THE WINE WAS NOTHING COMPARED TO BARFING FROM MY MOM. I WILL GET OFF THIS BUS AND SHE WILL NOT SAY ONE WORD TO ME.

OUR FATHER WHO ART IN HEAVEN AT LEAST NOW I GOT MY ANSWER OF WHY SHE DOESN'T WANT ME HERE.
TICKETS →
GREYHOU

OUR FATHER WHO ART IN HEAVEN, IT WAS MY FAULT FOR EVEN ASKING.
HOUND

REPORT ON LOVE

BY LYNDA "CELINA Y RENTILIO" BARRY © 1990

LOVE. WHAT IS IT? IT'S SUPPOSED TO BE BEAUTIFUL BUT LOVE CAN BE CRUDDY. LIKE YOU LOVING SOMEONE WHO DOES NOT LOVE YOU. THEN YOU WANT TO DO A SURGERY ON YOURSELF TO GET RID OF IT.

OR IF SOMEONE YOU JUST LIKE STARTS BEING ALL IN LOVE. THEN YOU GOT A HARD SITUATION. YOU HOPE IT WILL WEAR OFF THEM BEFORE THEY HATE YOU. THEN THERE'S WHERE YOU THOUGHT IT WAS LOVE BUT IT TURNS OUT NOT. BOTH PEOPLE FEEL EMBARRASSED AND HAVE TO HAVE DISCUSSIONS.

OR WHEN YOU LOVE THEM BUT ALL THE THINGS THEY DO STARTS GETTING ON YOUR NERVES LIKE THE WAY THEY CHEW FOOD AND YOU WONDER ARE THEY THINKING THE SAME THING ABOUT YOU WHICH THEY PROBABLY ARE. OR NO LOVE AT ALL FOR SO LONG THAT YOU THINK SOMETHING'S WRONG WITH YOU IN EVERY WAY.

I HAVE HAD THE GORGEOUS FEELING OF LOVE BUT MAINLY I HAVE HAD THE CRUDDY FEELING OF LOVE. ALL AROUND THE WORLD I BET IT IS THE SAME. CRUD IS THE MOST NORMAL FEELING. THEY SHOULD WRITE THAT IN THE SKY SO PEOPLE WILL KNOW IT AND NOT FEEL SO BAD.

REVERSE REVERSE
by LYNDA "MOVING VIOLATION" BARRY © 1990
I'M SO DEPRESSED. I FEEL SO BAD. I FEEL STUPID FOR EVEN WRITING THIS BECAUSE I KNOW THERE'S PEOPLE WITH WAY WORSE LIVES. I DON'T EVEN KNOW WHAT'S WRONG BECAUSE THERE'S NOTHING WRONG. EXCEPT MY ENTIRE PERSONALITY.
GUESS WHAT?
HEY.
GUESS WHAT?

DO YOU EVER GET THAT THING OF LOOKING IN THE MIRROR AND SAYING "STARTING NOW THINGS WILL BE DIFFERENT." YOU MAKE THE PROMISES: I WILL DO BETTER ON ALL THINGS. I WILL BE MORE INTERESTING. I WILL STOP LETTING DOUG MAKE OUT WITH ME WHEN EVER HE WANTS. STARTING NOW. STARTING RIGHT NOW. DEAR GOD CHANGE EVERYTHING. HERE IS MY PERMISSION SLIP.

THAT SONG "OH HOW I WISH THAT IT WOULD RAIN" IS PLAYING ON THE RADIO EXCEPT IT IS RAINING. SOMETIMES I WONDER: WHY KEEP LIVING? BUT THEN HOW WOULD I KILL MYSELF? I'M NOT INTO JUMPING OFF OF BUILDINGS. I'M NOT INTO DROWNING. I DON'T WANT TO CUT MY WRISTS BECAUSE I HATE CUTS. CHOKING? NO. CARBON MONOXIDE? TOO NOTICEABLE. HOW????

GREAT, RIGHT?

THAT'S MY GREAT NEW SAYING.

GUESS WHAT? CHICKEN BUTT!

I INVENTED IT.

SLEEPING PILLS IS THE #1 WAY. I FEEL SO INCREDIBLY INCREDIBLY INCREDIBLY TERRIBLE. PEOPLE THINK I'M BEING A BITCH. HOW CAN I EXPLAIN IT?? THERE IS NOTHING WRONG THAT I CAN PROVE TO ANYONE. JUST THIS FEELING. OH FORGET IT. FORGET I SAID ANYTHING.
UH-OH.
YOU'RE RIDING ON ANOTHER BUMMER AGAIN AREN'T YOU?

SOMETHING REAL

BY LYNDA STUFFY HEADED BARRY ©1990

I ASKED CINDY LUDERMYER DID SHE EVER WANT TO KILL HERSELF. SHE SAID "OH YEAH, ALL OF THE TIME." SHE SAID ONE TIME SHE ALMOST DID IT BY TAKING A WHOLE BOTTLE OF FLAVOR ORANGE ASPIRINS BUT THEN SHE BARFED IT OUT AT THE LAST MINUTE.

SHE KNEW HER MOM WOULD KILL HER IF SHE COMMITTED SUICIDE. I SAID BUT YOU'D ALREADY BE DEAD. SHE SAID SHE THOUGHT HER MOM COULD LOCATE HER ANYWAY. I WONDER WHO WOULD REALLY CARE IF I KILLED MYSELF. ALSO, WHAT'S IT LIKE TO BE DEAD? WHAT IF YOU JUST HAVE TO LAY THERE? SERIOUSLY?

I DOUBT THAT YOU GO FLYING AROUND AND I DOUBT YOU GO DOWN INTO HELL. TO DIE EQUALS WHAT? MY AUNT WILDA HAS SLEEPING PILLS. I HELD THE BOTTLE IN MY HAND. I THOUGHT THEY WOULD BE ACTUAL PILLS BUT THEY'RE MORE LIKE CONTACTS. WHAT WOULD I SAY IN MY NOTE? DEAR EVERYBODY.

THE MAIN THING I WOULD NOT WANT IS FOR MARLYS TO SEE ME AFTER I WAS DEAD. SHE ALREADY HAS BOMB NIGHTMARES AND DAD NIGHTMARES AND MOM NIGHTMARES. I DON'T WANT TO ADD SISTER ONES. I WILL HAVE TO PLAN IT OUT SO CAREFUL. I GUESS YOU CAN TELL THAT SOMETHING'S REAL WHEN YOU CAN'T BELIEVE YOU'RE ACTUALLY DOING IT.

I GOT LOGICAL

BY LYNDA BARRY ©1990

OK. I DIDN'T DO IT. WHY? BECAUSE AT THE LAST MINUTE IT TURNS OUT I AM CHICKEN TO KILL MYSELF. AT THE LAST MINUTE I WAS THINKING HOW I KNOW IT WOULD BE GREAT TO HAVE ALL MY PROBLEMS GONE BUT **HOW COULD I EVEN NOTICE IT IF I WAS DEAD?** I GOT LOGICAL **ON MYSELF.**

NOW IT'S MORNING AND I AM GETTING READY FOR SCHOOL. I AM STARING AT MARLYS WHO IS TELLING ME A JOKE. (Q) WHY IS SIX AFRAID OF SEVEN? (A) BECAUSE 7 8 9. IF I WAS DEAD I WOULD NEVER HAVE HEARD THAT JOKE OR SEEN MARLYS NOW DANCING TO THE SONG SOUL FINGER THAT'S COMING **OUT OF OUR RADIO. THE TREE OUTSIDE OUR WINDOW HAS LEAVES ALL BRIGHT GREEN. I WOULD HAVE NEVER** SEEN THOSE LEAVES.

DOWNSTAIRS MY GRANDMA YELLS IT'S BREAKFAST. SLANTS OF SUN ARE LANDING ON THE WALLS. FOR THE FIRST TIME IN FOREVER MY HAIR DOESN'T LOOK WARPED. THE SMELL COMES IN THE ROOM OF PAN-CAKES. NOW MARLYS IS SINGING VIVA LAS VEGAS. "COME ON!" SHE SAYS AND I FOLLOW HER. AT THE TABLE GRANDMA TELLS US MR. LUDERMYER HAD A HEART ATTACK LAST NIGHT. THEY DON'T KNOW IF HE IS GOING TO MAKE IT.

I SEE HER EYES ALL RED. THROUGH THE WINDOWS MORE SUN, MORE SUN, SUD-DENLY BRIGHTER AND BRIGHTER UNTIL MY VIEW GOES WHITE. IS HE STILL LOOKING OUT HIS EYES OR DID HE FLY UP INVISIBLE INTO PITCH BLACK? GRANDMA CALLS THE HOSPITAL. THEY TELL HER HE IS STILL HANGING ON. WHY IS SIX AFRAID OF SEVEN. WHEN HE COMES HOME I WILL TELL HIM.

HELP YOU

by LYNDA "NEW WAY OF WALKING" BARRY © 1990

NOW IS THE TIME FOR ALL GOOD MEN. NOW IS THE TIME FOR ALL GOOD MEN TO COME TO THE AID OF GOD I HATE THIS CLASS I HATE TYPING SO MUCH. NEXT TO ME IS WHERE CINDY LUDERMYER SITS. USUALLY. USUALLY, BEFORE HER DAD'S HEART ATTACK. FOUR DAYS AGO AND THEY STILL DON'T KNOW WILL HE MAKE IT.

WE HAD TO EXPLAIN TO MARLYS WHAT'S A HEART ATTACK. THEN SHE GOT SCARED THAT HERS WOULD START ATTACKING. "NO" MY GRANDMA SAID. "THAT'S ONLY WHEN YOU'RE OLD." MARLYS SAID "HOW OLD?" NOW SHE WANTS US TO CALL DAD. BUT WHO EVEN KNOWS WHERE DAD IS? CALL ANY PHONE BOOTH NUMBER ANYWHERE AND MAYBE HE'LL PICK UP. I TOLD HER NO WAY DID OUR DAD HAVE A HEART ATTACK ALSO. THAT WOULD BE JUST TOO MUCH A COINCIDENCE FOR REALITY.

DEAR SIR, I AM WRITING TO INQUIRE ABOUT A POSITION IN YOUR COMPANY. MY QUALIFICATIONS ARE AS FOLLOWS IF DAD DID GET A HEART ATTACK HOW WOULD WE KNOW? IT'S HOW MY GRANDFATHER DIED. MY GRANDMOTHER SAID HE WAS EATING HIS DINNER WHEN IT JUST CAME. DEAR MR. SMITH, THANK YOU FOR YOUR PROMPT RESPONSE TO MY LETTER OF SEPTEMBER 2 OUR FATHER WHO ART IN HEAVEN PLEASE DON'T LET MR. LUDERMYER DIE. DEAR CINDY I AM SENDING YOU AN ESP FROM TYPING I AM PRAYING FOR YOUR DAD.

BOTH GIRLS.

IS THAT RIGHT.

AND DEAR DAD I AM SENDING YOU AN ESP TOO COULD YOU PLEASE CALL US. JUST CALL US JUST CALL US JUST CALL US. IT'S FOR MARLYS BECAUSE SHE IS FREAKING OUT. I AM USED TO FREAKING OUT BUT SHE IS NOT. SO JUST CALL US. THE QUICK BROWN FOX JUMPED OVER THE LAZY DOG. DO NOT LOOK DOWN AT THE KEYS. DEAR MR. AND MRS. LEE, WE ARE HAPPY TO INFORM YOU I CAN'T CONCENTRATE. HAIL MARY FULL OF GRACE PLEASE LET HIM BE O.K. R.S.V.P. THANK YOU, YOURS TRULY, MAYBONNE MAYDELLE MULLEN. SINCERELY, MISS MAYBONNE M. MULLEN.

HELP YOU?
YEAH.
SCOTCH ROCKS.

WHERE EVER YOU ARE
by Lynda Supercalafragalistic BARRY © 1990
HAVE YOU EVER READ THE GUINNESS BOOK OF WORLD RECORDS? BOY WHAT A GREAT BOOK. WHEN MR. LUDERMYER CAME HOME FROM HIS HEART ATTACK I GOT IT FOR HIM AS A GET BETTER PRESENT.
OK, NOW BLUEY,

THAT'S THE MAIN THING ME AND HIM HAVE IN COMMON. WE BOTH LOVE INTEREST AND WE BOTH LOVE FACTS. JIM MONTE-CINO PLAYED THE PIANO FOR 7 DAYS AND 8 3/4 HOURS STRAIGHT IN THE TROCADERO BALL ROOM IN AUCKLAND, NEW ZEALAND IN 1951. DON'T YOU WISH YOU COULD HAVE BEEN THERE TO CLAP FOR HIM?

HERE'S YOUR DINNER OLD BOY

MY FRIENDS SAY I THINK I'M AN ENCYCLOPEDIA BECAUSE OF MY FACTS. THEY THINK I'M SHOWING OFF BUT TO ME FACTS ARE AS GORGEOUS AS THE MOST GORGEOUS OF MUSIC. THERE ARE OVER ONE MILLION TUBES IN THE HUMAN KIDNEY. ALL THE PLANETS IN THE SOLAR SYSTEM CAN FIT INSIDE JUPITER. DEAN MARTIN WEARS A SIZE 12 SHOE.

MR. LUDERMYER SAYS I UNDERSTAND HIM BETTER THAN HIS WIFE. I WAS IN HIS ROOM READING HIM THE GUINESS BOOK. I READ HIM ABOUT THE DOG NAMED BLUEY WHO GUARDED THE SHEEP FOR HIS MASTER FOR 29 YEARS. WORLD'S OLDEST DOG. "SON OF A BITCH MUSTA FELL APART WHEN THAT DOG PASSED AWAY" MR. LUDERMYER SAID, THEN HE STARTED CRYING AND I DON'T KNOW WHY BUT I STARTED CRYING TOO. I'M GLAD MR. LUDERMYER IS BETTER. DEAR BLUEY. HELLO FROM ME AND MR. LUDERMYER WHERE EVER YOU ARE.

MARLYS SPRING

BY LYNDA BARRY ✿ FOR GARY COVINO ✿ © 1990

I SHARE THE BED WITH MY LITTLE SISTER MARLYS WHO SOMETIMES JUST KILLS ME. LIKE THIS MORNING SHE WAS SINGING JERIMIAH WAS A BULLFROG OUT THE OPEN WINDOW OF OUR BEDROOM.

IT WAS THE FIRST WARM DAY OF THE YEAR. IN THE FRONT YARD THERE WERE FLOWERS. SHE SAID DID I DARE HER TO GO OUT ON THE ROOF AND DO THE BUTT DANCE IN HER PAJAMAS. THIS IS THE DANCE WHERE YOU STICK YOUR BUTT OUT AS MUCH AS POSSIBLE. SHE INVENTED IT.

SHE CLIMBS OUT THE WINDOW AND STARTS SINGING LA CUCARACHA THEN SHE BENDS OVER AND SINGS "SOMEONE LEFT THE CAKE OUT IN THE RAIN." A CAR HONKS AT HER AND SHE STICKS HER ARM IN THE AIR AND SHOUTS "BLACK POWER!" THEN THE DOOR FLIES OPEN AND IT'S MY GRANDMA YELLING IS MARLYS TRYING TO KILL HER?

OH BABY
COME ON
LET ME TAKE
YOU WHERE
THE ACTION IS

MARLYS!

3656

AT BREAKFAST MY GRANDMA WON'T SHUT UP ABOUT HOW I HAVE NO RESPONSIBILITY. HOW COULD I LET MY SISTER BEHAVE THAT WAY, SHE COULD HAVE FALLEN OFF THE ROOF AND WHAT ABOUT THE NEIGHBORS. THEN SHE TURNS HER HEAD TO GET THE TOAST, AND MARLYS LOOKS AT ME AND SMILES. MAN. I NEVER KNEW I LOVED HER SO MUCH.

MESSED UP + CONFUSED
LYNDA BARRY ©1990
DEAR ABBY. FIRST I THINK YOU ARE SO GREAT WITH ALL YOUR ADVICE OF PROBLEMS. OK. HERE IS MY DEAL. THERE IS THIS NEW GUY WHO LIKES ME. HIS NAME IS DAVID BRANICA. HE HAS DEVELOPED HUMOR, IS VERY UNIQUE, HE PLAYS GUITAR AND HAS A 2.8 GPA.
YOU HATE ME, RIGHT?

HE HAS INCREDIBLE EYELASHES AND I HAVE FELT ATTRACTED TO HIM SINCE THE FIRST DAY OF CONTEMPORARY PROBLEMS EVEN THOUGH IN A WAY HE IS STRAIGHTER THAN ME AND IN A WAY HE IS MORE INNOCENT THAN ME. WAY MORE INNOCENT. THAT IS PART ONE OF THE PROBLEM. I USED TO BE INNOCENT.

I KNOW YOU DO.

BUT I MET THIS GUY DOUG BACK AT THE BEGINNING OF THE YEAR AND IT'S HARD TO EXPLAIN BUT DOUG WAS ADVANCED AND THEN FROM KNOWING HIM I GOT ADVANCED TOO. I MEAN IT WAS PHYSICAL. THEN DOUG TREATED ME LIKE TRASH BUT IT TOOK A LONG TIME BEFORE I NOTICED IT. I JUST THOUGHT YOUR BOYFRIEND BEING A CRUD WAS NORMAL.

NO I DON'T.

YOU DON'T?

NOW I GOT DAVID WHO IS NICE BUT I AM SLIGHTLY FREAKING OUT. IF WE GO PHYSICAL THEN WILL HE TURN COLD BLOODED AFTERWARDS? AND WHEN HE FINDS OUT THAT I ACCIDENTLY GOT ADVANCED BEFORE HE COULD BE THE ONE TO ADVANCE ME, WILL HE TURN COLD BLOODED THEN? PLEASE ANSWER SOON.
I AM: *Messed up and Confused.*

WILL YOU GO MAIL THIS LETTER FOR ME?
SURE!

DO YOU BELIEVE IN MAGIC

by LYNDA BARRY ©1990

SUE ACKER HAD A PARTY, MY FIRST ONE I WENT TO WITH ME AND DAVID AS A COUPLE. IT WAS IN HER FAMOUS BASEMENT. JUST RED LIGHT BULBS AND BEAN BAG CHAIRS PLUS 100 MELLOW CORNERS FOR MAKING OUT. HER PARENTS ARE UNITARIANS WITH FREE MINDS.

THERE WAS ALL THE PERFECT SONGS OF CRYSTAL BLUE PERSUASION, IT'S A BEAUTIFUL MORNING AND LA LA MEANS I LOVE YOU SO YOU KNOW ME AND DAVID WERE SLOW DANCING. THE ODORS OF HIS BRUT COLOGNE WAS BLOWING MY MIND AWAY AND THE FEELING OF HIS FINGERS ON MY BACK. YOU KNOW THAT GREAT CAR-STOMACH FEELING WHEN YOU FLY OVER A HUMP? THAT WAS MY WHOLE BODY.

HE PUT HIS LIPS BY MY EAR, I FELT THE BREATH FROM HIS NOSE AND THE BUCKLE ON HIS BELT DUG ME. THAT THING WHERE WORDS CANNOT EXPLAIN WAS FLOWING AND THEY PUT ON THE SONG "WHEN THE WIND CRIES MARY" THEN DAVID EXPLODED THE WINDMILLS OF MY MIND BY KISSING ME KISSING ME KISSING ME. AND I WAS SHAKING. AND ALL THE BAD THINGS IN MY LIFE TURNED TO WORTH IT.

YOU CAN NEVER TELL WHEN THE BEAUTIFUL MAGIC OF LIFE WILL HAPPEN TO YOU. YOU CAN NEVER TELL WHEN ALL THE STARS WILL FALL FROM THE SKY.

MY PROBLEM
BY LYNDA BARRY © 1990
I THINK I GOT AN INFERIORITY COMPLEX. SUE ACKER EXPLAINED ME THE CONCEPT TODAY AT LUNCH. WHERE YOU HAVE FEELINGS OF SECRET CRUDDINESS AROUND EVERYONE. I JUST THOUGHT THAT WAS NORMAL LIFE!
MILK

SUE SAID YOU CURE IT BY JUST BEING YOURSELF BECAUSE INSIDE EVERYONE IS BEAUTIFUL. I SAID EVEN HITLER? HE WAS BEING HIMSELF. SHE SAID NO. HE WAS ACTING SELF CONSCIOUS AND COULD I QUIT TALKING ABOUT HITLER BECAUSE I WAS BRINGING PEOPLE DOWN. SHE SAID WHY DO I ALWAYS WANT TO BRING EVERYONE DOWN TO THE LEVEL OF MY BUMMER?

SUE SAID SHE THINKS I NEED A TRUTH SESSION. I GO, "WHAT'S THAT?" IT'S WHERE EVERYONE GETS IN A CIRCLE AROUND YOU IN HER BASEMENT AND ADMITS THINGS ABOUT YOUR PERSONALITY. ONLY PEOPLE WHO ARE CHICKEN TO EVOLVE WON'T DO IT. "DO YOU WANT TO EVOLVE?" SHE SAID.

SHE WARNED ME THAT IF I DIDN'T CURE MY INFERIORITY COMPLEX I WOULD LOSE ALL MY FRIENDS AND ALSO DAVID AS MY BOYFRIEND. "IT'S YOUR WHOLE PROBLEM." SHE SAID, "YOUR PERSONALITY."
I WATCHED HER EAT THE REST OF HER SANDWICH, AND THEN THE BELL RANG.
MY TRUTH SESSION IS ON FRIDAY.

the PLASTIC WALL
by LYNDA EVER LOVIN' BARRY © 1990!
EVER SINCE I FOUND OUT I HAVE A INFERIORITY COMPLEX I HAVE BEEN FEELING SO TERRIBLE. ALSO, MORE SELF-CONSCIOUS THAN MY LIFE HAS EVER KNOWN.

IT'S A THING WHERE I WISH I COULDN'T TALK BECAUSE EVERYTHING I SAY IS SO STUPID BUT I CAN'T CONTROL MY MOUTH. IT KEEPS OPENING AND BORING THINGS COME OUT. ALSO I HAVE NOTICED I AM UGLY COMPARED TO ALL MY FRIENDS. OUT OF EVERYONE IT TURNS OUT I AM THE DOG. I'M NOT SAYING THIS ONLY TO GET ATTENTION. I'M REALIZING FACTS.

THERE'S ALSO GOOD QUALITIES. READING COMPREHENSION, ARTISTIC AND NOT TO SOUND CONCEITED BUT GOOD AT POETRY. BUT HOW MUCH DOES THAT COUNT WHEN YOUR FACE + BODY + WHOLE PERSONALITY SUCKS? SUE ACKER AND THEM ARE GOING TO GIVE ME A TRUTH SESSION ON THE REALITY OF THEIR OPINIONS ON ME WHICH SHE SAYS WORKED GOOD ON HER COUSIN CAROL FROM IDAHO. I HOPE IT WORKS FOR ME.

MOST OF ALL I JUST WISH FOR EVERYTHING ABOUT ME TO CHANGE. AND THEN I SWEAR TO GOD I WOULD QUIT ACTING INSECURE, AND BE MYSELF, LIKE IN ALL THE SONGS WHERE PEOPLE ARE BEING THEMSELVES. I WOULD STOP FAKING AND BE. FOR REAL AND ACT FREE LIKE SUE ACKER AND THEM, BECAUSE FOR RIGHT NOW I AM ONLY A PLASTIC WALL OF ILLUSION, WHICH I HATE. IF I HAVE A POSSIBILITY TO CHANGE, PLEASE GOD LET IT HAPPEN.

OR SOMETHING

LYNDA steady Rock Barry © 1990

WELL, SUE ACKER AND THEM DID THE TRUTH SESSION THING TO ME TODAY AND I DIDN'T START CRYING UNTIL CINDY LUDERMYER GAVE HER COMMENT OF HOW I LET DOUG USE ME ALL HE WANTED AND HOW I PLAYED MYSELF FOR CHEAP WITH HIM WHICH IS SUCH A JOKE CONSIDERING WHAT A KNOWN SLUT CINDY LUDERMYER IS WITH DOUG.

SHE THINKS IT DOESN'T COUNT BECAUSE HE GAVE HER THAT UGLY RING BUT HE STILL TREATS HER LIKE A DOG. NO RING CAN MAKE YOU NOT A SLUT. I TOLD CINDY "YOU'RE THE EXACT SAME AS ME AND YOU KNOW IT." WHICH WAS BREAKING THE TRUTH SESSION RULE OF NO TALKING BACK BUT I COULDN'T HELP IT THEN CINDY STARTED CRYING. I THOUGHT IT WAS FAKE CRYING TO GET MERCY.

SHE SAID "IT DOESN'T EVEN MATTER. I KNOW YOU ALL SECRETLY HATE ME ANYWAY" WHICH WE ALL SAID BACK "NO WE DON'T" THEN I REALIZED SHE WAS CRYING FOR REAL BECAUSE NO ONE WOULD FAKE THEIR NOSE LETTING OUT A GIGANTOR DRIP WHICH EVERYONE SAW. I FELT SO TERRIBLE. I SAID "CINDY, MAN I AM SORRY." THEN THE WEIRDEST THING HAPPENED. SHE SAID SHE WAS SORRY FOR BEING SO MEAN TO ME SINCE I MOVED HERE.

PUSH FOR WALK LIGHT

I DIDN'T EVEN KNOW SHE WAS BEING MEAN! I JUST THOUGHT THAT WAS HER NATURAL PERSONALITY! THEN SHE GOES "I HATE MYSELF SO MUCH I SHOULD COMMIT SUICIDE", THEN I SAID "DON'T DO IT BECAUSE YOU'RE GREAT." AND OTHER PEOPLE WERE CRYING THEN EVERYONE WAS CRYING THEN MRS. ACKER CAME DOWN THE STAIRS AND FREAKED OUT AT OUR EMOTIONS AND SAID FOR US TO GO HOME. ME AND CINDY WALKED TOGETHER. AND NOW I GUESS WE'RE FRIENDS. OR SOMETHING.

HEY MAYBONNE.
YEAH?
WANNA COME OVER?

CAN I BE EXCUSED?
by LYNDA BARRY © 1990
IT IS WEIRD BEING FRIENDS WITH SOMEONE YOU USED TO HATE. IT'S EMBARRASSING. LIKE IF THEY ACCIDENTLY START TELLING ABOUT A PARTY THEY DIDN'T INVITE YOU TO, AND THEN IN THE MIDDLE THEY HAVE TO SUDDENLY LOOK DOWN. AND THEN YOU HAVE TO SAY "THAT'S OK."
THAT'S OK.

WITH ME AND CINDY, THE REALITY SHE THINKS IS HAPPENING IS THAT THE WHOLE TIME SHE WAS HATING ME, SHE THOUGHT I WAS LIKING HER AND WISHING SHE WAS MY FRIEND. ONE PART OF THAT REALITY IS TRUE. I WISHED SHE WAS MY FRIEND BECAUSE IF CINDY HATES YOU, YOU DON'T GET INVITED NOWHERE.

THE PART TWO OF THAT REALITY, THOUGH, IS THAT I NEVER DID LIKE CINDY. THAT'S *MY* TOO EMBARRASSING FACT WHEN WE TALK. DOES IT EQUAL A LIE IF YOU DON'T *TELL* A LIE, YOU JUST NEVER SAY THE ACTUAL TRUTH OF YOUR FEELINGS? IF I TOLD HER, IT COULD MESS EVERYTHING UP BECAUSE RIGHT NOW SHE IS BEING SO NICE TO ME BECAUSE SHE IS SO SORRY.

DON'T EVEN WORRY ABOUT IT NO MORE.

I KNOW SHE THINKS I'M INNOCENT OF HATRED WHICH I SWEAR TO GOD *IS* MY PERFECT GOAL SO IN A WAY IT IS *TRUE*, AT LEAST IN THE FUTURE. THE MAIN THING I DON'T KNOW IS WHEN SHE KEEPS SAYING I'M SORRY, AM I A CHUMP THAT IS JUST PLAYING WITH HER MIND? OR CAN I, FOR THIS ONE TIME, JUST PLEASE BE EXCUSED?

SERIOUSLY. JUST FORGET ABOUT IT.

I HAVE DESIRES

BY · LYNDA BARRY · © 1990

THERE'S A GUY LIKING ME, DAVID BRANICA, WELL YOU KNOW HE IS WONDERFUL. NANCY NEWBY AND SUE ACKER AND THEM SAY I AM A LUCKY DOG.

BUT HOW CAN I EXPLAIN IT? I KNOW HE IS PERFECT IN EVERY WAY AND IF YOU CAN BELIEVE IT, HE LIKES SOUL MUSIC WHICH NO PEOPLE OUT HERE DO. WHEN WE TALK, I KNOW HIS FEELINGS AND WHEN WE KISS HE DOESN'T GO UP MY BRA. BUT IS IT BAD THAT I WANT HIM TO? HE THINKS I AM SO GOOD.

ON THE PEACH TREE THERE ARE FLOWERS. ON THE APPLE TREE PLUM TREE AND CHERRY. IN THE MORNING WHEN I WALK TO SCHOOL, I KEEP SEEING THE BEAUTIFUL DETAILS. I KEEP SMELLING THE BEAUTIFUL OXYGEN. HE DOESN'T FRENCH. HE WANTS PEACE AND ECOLOGY. BUT THINK ABOUT IF I FRENCH HIM ON ACCIDENT? I'M BUSTED.

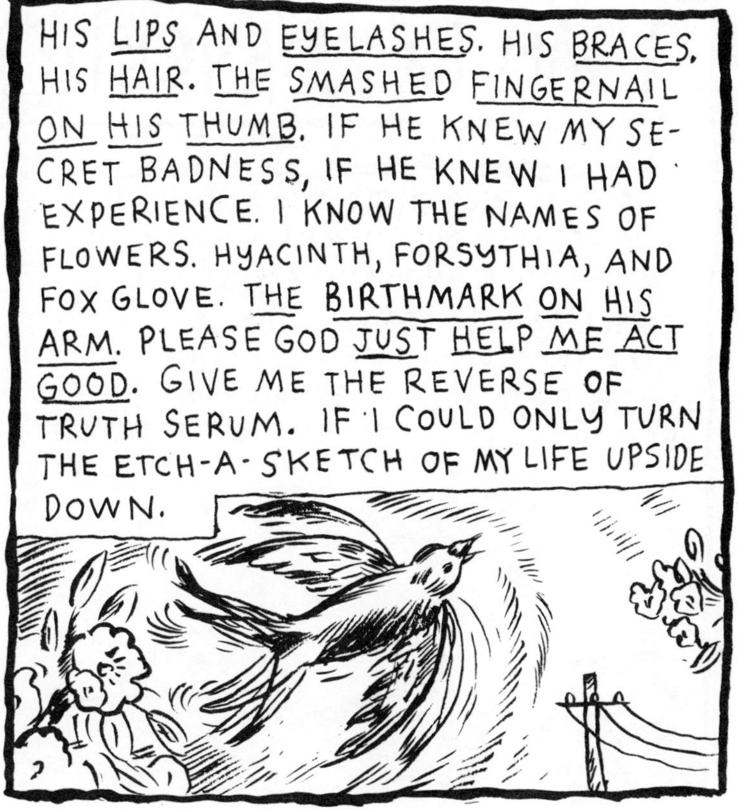

HIS LIPS AND EYELASHES. HIS BRACES. HIS HAIR. THE SMASHED FINGERNAIL ON HIS THUMB. IF HE KNEW MY SECRET BADNESS, IF HE KNEW I HAD EXPERIENCE. I KNOW THE NAMES OF FLOWERS. HYACINTH, FORSYTHIA, AND FOX GLOVE. THE BIRTHMARK ON HIS ARM. PLEASE GOD JUST HELP ME ACT GOOD. GIVE ME THE REVERSE OF TRUTH SERUM. IF I COULD ONLY TURN THE ETCH-A-SKETCH OF MY LIFE UPSIDE DOWN.

I AM EXPERIENCED

by Lynda Barry © 1990

DAVID IS SO INCREDIBLE AND ALSO HE HAS AN INCREDIBLE DOG KNUCKLES WHO CAN JUMP HIGH UP AND CATCH A SUPERBALL. HE ASKED ME TO COME WITH HIM TO A PLACE THAT WOULD TRIP MY MIND OUT. I ALREADY TOLD YOU HE'S NOT THAT EX-PERIENCED.

HE KNOWS A HOLE IN THE GOLF COURSE FENCE. HE WALKED ME TO WHERE YOU CAN'T SEE NO MORE CIVILIZATION, ONLY PURE GRASS AND PURE TREES, AND HE GAVE ME A FEELING WHEN HE SAID: WHAT IF RIGHT NOW WE WERE ADAM AND EVE AND HOW HE WANTED TO GET EXPERIENCED.

HIS ARMS WENT AROUND ME THEN KISSING, THEN I COULDN'T HELP IT, I FRENCHED HIM, THEN HE FRENCHES AND STARTS PULLING MY SHIRT OUT, HIS COLD HANDS GOING UP SO INCREDIBLY, WHICH WOULD HAVE BEEN PERFECT EXCEPT FOR KNUCKLES DIDN'T BARK THE WARNING. WE DIDN'T SEE THE GUARD MAN UNTIL IT WAS TOO LATE TO RUN.

HE YELLED OUT ALL THE THINGS WE HAD NO BUSINESS DOING. DIDN'T WE RESPECT PRIVATE PROPERTY, AND DID I WANT TO GET PREGNANT BECAUSE THAT WAS MY DIRECTION, AND IF I WAS HIS DAUGHTER HE'D BEAT THE HELL OUT OF ME. AND MY FACE WAS BURNING. BURNING HOT. AFTER THAT, WALKING HOME, THE FEELING WAS DIFFERENT. AFTER THAT, WALKING HOME, DAVID WOULDN'T EVEN HOLD MY HAND.

SEE YOU

XBXYXLXYXNXDXA "WHERE DID I LAY MY PUTTY KNIFE" BARRY © '90

DAVID. HE WAS MY BOYFRIEND. AT LEAST HE THOUGHT SO AND EVERYONE AT SCHOOL THOUGHT SO TOO. BUT THEN, I DON'T KNOW. BRENDA TOLD ME ONE TIME THAT THIS THING HAPPENS WHEN GUYS ARE NICE. WHEN GUYS ARE NICE, YOUR FEELINGS CAN JUST SORT OF STOP.

HE CAME UP TO ME AT MY LOCKER AND MY EYES COULDN'T LOOK AT HIM. IT WAS A PRESENT FOR ME IN HIS HANDS. A BLACK VELVET CAT WITH YELLOW DIAMOND EYES IN A PLASTIC DOME WITH PERFUME. "THANKS" I SAID. "IT'S GREAT." HE KEPT STANDING THERE.

ON HIS FOLDER I SAW MY NAME IN DRAWN LETTERS. "YOU STILL ON PHONE RESTRICTION?" HE SAID. I HAD TOLD HIM THIS LIE. "YEAH" I SAID. "KIND OF." THE BELL RANG. "I'LL WALK YOU" HE SAID. "YOU'LL GET LATE" I SAID. "BIG DEAL" HE SAID. "BIG FAT DEAL." WE CROSSED UNDER THE BREEZEWAY, NOT TALKING.

AT HOME EC I SAY "WELL. SEE YA." HE KEEPS STANDING THERE. THE LAST BELL RINGS. HE STARES AT ME. "OK" HE FINALLY SAYS. "OK." I SAY BACK. THEN HE SAYS SOFT: "YOU STILL LIKE ME, RIGHT?" MY MOUTH MADE THE LIE. "YEAH. SURE." I SAY. "OK!" HE SAYS. I WATCH HIM RUN THE HALL. HE RUNS IT AND AT THE CORNER DOES THE MOVE OF A JUMPSHOT, BOTH HANDS TO THE CEILING.

JUST FORGET

LYNDA "NATIONAL BADEMA OF MALI" BARRY © 1990

I WAS AT CINDY LUDERMYER'S. UP IN HER ROOM. "HE'S STILL THERE" SHE SAYS. OUT THE WINDOW IS DAVID WAITING FOR ME BY THE TREE. "HE CAN'T TAKE A HINT" CINDY SAYS.

AT DINNER MY GRANDMA SAYS. "EVERY TIME I LOOK OUTSIDE HE'S THERE. WHAT ARE YOU MIXED UP IN?" "NOTHING" I SAY. SHE STARES AT ME. MY SISTER SAYS "HE LOVES HER BUT SHE DOESN'T LOVE HIM BACK." THE DOORBELL. I'M BUSTED. THE STUPID DOOR'S OPEN AND HE CAN SEE ME THROUGH THE SCREEN. "HEY MAY-BONNE" HE SAYS. "CAN YOU COME OUT?"

"YOU'RE NOT GOING ANYWHERE" MY GRANDMA SAYS. "JUST IN THE YARD" I SAY. "10 MINUTES. THAT'S IT" SHE TELLS ME, AND THEN LOUD SO I KNOW HE HEARS: "YOU TELL THAT BOY I DON'T WANT HIM BY THE HOUSE ANYMORE." I OPEN THE SCREEN DOOR. "HEY DAVID" I SAY.

WE LEAN ON MY GRANDMA'S CAR. MY MOUTH WON'T SAY ANYTHING AND I FEEL NERVOUS. HE STARES AT ME. THE STREET LIGHTS COME ON. THEN MY GRANDMA'S VOICE SHOUTING MY NAME. "I GOTTA GO" I SAY. HE KEEPS STARING. "OK, SEE YOU" I SAY AND TURN. "SO JUST FORGET IT, RIGHT?" HE SAYS. "JUST FORGET THE WHOLE THING, RIGHT?" HIS FIST POUNDS THE CAR AND I LOOK DOWN. AND THEN HE IS WALKING FAST. AND THEN HE IS GONE.

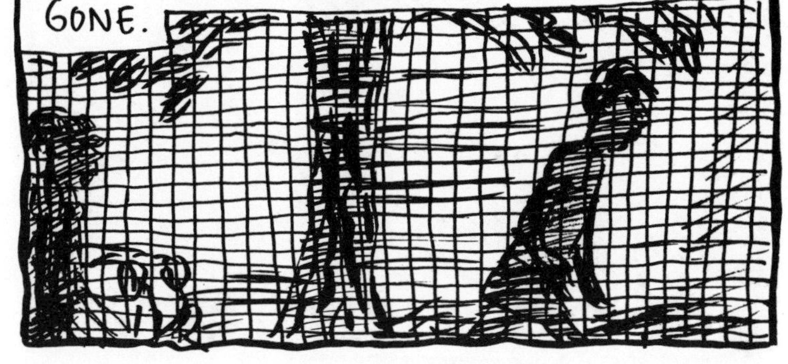

WHAT IT IS

by L Y N D A B A R R Y © 1990

DEAR BRENDA WHAT IT IS. I GOT YOUR LETTER THAT WAS AMAZING ABOUT YOU AND PAUL! ALL RIGHT! TOMORROW'S THE LAST DAY OF SCHOOL SO MANY PEOPLE ARE SUPPOSED TO GET BEAT UP. THERE'S SO MANY WARPED PEOPLE HERE. ALSO ONLY 9th grade gets a PARTY.

GUESS WHAT ME AND DAVID ARE BROKEN UP NOW. LIKE I TOLD YOU HE WAS A BEAUTIFUL PERSON BUT YOU KNOW THAT THING OF HOW a GUY STARTS GETTING ON YOUR NERVES. EVERYTHING THEY DO. I WROTE HIM a POEM EXPLAINING IT IN A LETTER BUT I DOUBT HE GETS IT. HEY GUESS WHAT I GOT A JOB.

IT'S AT THE ROYAL THEATER OWNED BY THE UNCLE OF THAT GIRL I TOLD YOU ABOUT CINDY LUDERMYER. I KNOW THAT'S WEIRD, RIGHT? BECAUSE I WROTE YOU SHE WAS COLD AND ALL SNOBBISH BUT SHE'S NOT THAT BAD. WANT TO HEAR SOMETHING WEIRD SHE MIGHT NOT BE A VIRGIN BUT SHE DOESN'T KNOW FOR SURE. I'M IN MATH. THIS CLASS IS THE MOST BORING CLASS. THE TEACHER IS CRUSTY.

MY JOB'S SELLING POPCORN AND REFRESHMENTS. CINDY'S WORKING THERE TOO IT'S AN INCREDIBLE OPPORTUNITY. TO MEET CUTE GUYS THAT IS! HA-HA-HA. JUST JOKING BECAUSE SERIOUSLY I'M GOING TO BE VERY RESPONSIBLE. IT'S ALMOST THE BELL. A LOT OF PEOPLE ARE SKIPPING TOMORROW. NOT ME. I'M INTO THAT ONE BAND *BREAD* THAT ONE GUY'S VOICE IN "I FOUND YOUR DIARY UNDERNEATH A TREE."

WRITE BACK SOON! ☮ + LOVE

P.S. I AM SO BORED.

Maybonne

PPS. I AM STILL BORED.

FIRST DAY

by Lynda MATCHHEAD BARRY © 1990

I WAKE UP. FIRST THING I THINK IS "NO SCHOOL." THE SONG BY SLY IS ON THE CLOCK RADIO. MY SISTER IS ALREADY OUTSIDE, I HEAR HER YELLING IN THE FRONT YARD.

I DON'T MAKE TRASH LIKE YOU, I BURN IT!!!

ENDA THE SPRING AN' HERE SHE COMES BACK HI HI HI HI BABE

I LOOK OUT THE WINDOW. "SHUT UP!" I YELL AT MARLYS. "YOU!" SHE YELLS BACK. A KID I NEVER SAW BEFORE YELLS "HA-HA-HA! EVEN YOUR OWN SISTER SAYS SHUT UP TO YOU!" MARLYS SLUGS THE KID. HE SLUGS HER BACK. SHE RUNS IN THE HOUSE AND SCREAMS AT ME.

I HATE YOU!

SHUT UP!! I HATE YOU!

MY GRANDMOTHER YELLS "FOR THE LOVE OF GOD! KNOCK IT OFF!" I YELL "SHE WOKE ME UP!" MY GRANDMA YELLS "IT'S TIME TO GET UP ANYWAY! IT'S 10:30!" IF THERE WAS STILL SCHOOL, NORMALLY I WOULD BE IN MATH RIGHT NOW. I NOTICE THE BEAUTY OF LIFE AND I AM IN A PERFECT MOOD. I EAT SOME TOAST AND IT TASTES DELICIOUS. MARLYS TELLS ME ABOUT THE KID WHO SLUGGED HER AND SHE SOUNDS ACTUALLY INTERESTING TO ME.

HIS NAME IS RANDALL
HE THINKS HE'S BIG
HE'S A BUTT
HE'S TEDDY'S COUSIN
I TOLD HIM DON'T GET WISE BUBBLE EYES OR I'LL KNOCK YOU DOWN TO PEANUT SIZE.

OUT THE WINDOW I SEE CINDY ON THE BACK PORCH. I RUN ACROSS THE DRIVE-WAY IN MY BABY DOLLS. "DARE TO BE BARE!" CINDY SAYS. "WANNA GO TO THE POOL?" I SIT BY HER, LISTENING TO THE WHISPERED STORY OF HER AND HER BOYFRIEND SNEAKING OUT LAST NIGHT. IN THE YARD THE SPRINKLER SHOOTS UP A MILLION TINY SPARKS OF WATER. IT'S SUMMER. IT FINALLY FINALLY IS.

IF YOU WERE ME

LYNDA BARRY 1990

IT WAS A HOT NIGHT AT 11:00. I WAS STAYING OVERNIGHT AT CINDY'S. IN THE FRONT ROOM WAS MR. LUDERMYER IN HIS UNDERPANTS AND MRS. LUDERMYER SETTING HER RAW DENTURES ON THE END TABLE. THE TV WAS ON. A MUSIC SHOW WITH DEAN MARTIN TURNED UP LOUD.

HER PARENTS TELL US "NO TOM FOOLERY" AND GO TO BED. IN THE KITCHEN CINDY'S SENIOR HIGH BROTHER KEITH MAKES THE COMMENT OF WHY DO ALL HER FRIENDS HAVE NO BOOBS AND HIS FRIEND AGNER HITS THE TABLE LAUGHING SAYING "YEAH. COME ON CINDY"! I CAN SEE MY HOUSE THROUGH THE SCREEN DOOR. ALL THE LIGHTS ARE OFF.

UP IN CINDY'S ROOM WE CHANGE INTO PAJAMAS AND CINDY SAYS I'M SO LUCKY TO BE FLAT AND HOW SHE WISHES SHE WAS FLAT, THEN SHE PASSES ME KYPED VODKA FROM A JAR IN HER CLOSET AND WE GO BACK DOWNSTAIRS. ON THE COUCH ARE KEITH AND AGNER. EXCEPT FOR THE TV THERES NO LIGHTS. "WHAT'S THE MOVIE?" CINDY SAYS. "SOMETHING LAME" KEITH SAYS AND I SEE THE EYES OF AGNER CLIMB HER.

WE LAY ON THE RUG IN FRONT. ME ON MY STOMACH AND CINDY ON HER SIDE. THEN CINDY GOES IN THE KITCHEN AND THEN AGNER GOES IN THE KITCHEN. AND KEITH LAYS NEXT TO ME, ASKING ME THINGS. LITTLE THINGS. AND SAYING HOW EVER SINCE HE SAW ME HE ALWAYS THOUGHT I WAS NICE. REALLY NICE. THEN HIS HAND REACHES THE TV BUTTON, IT'S LIKE SLOW MOTION, AND THE WHOLE ROOM GOES BLACK.

DROPPING OUT

@ LYNDA "Laid in Jail" BARRY © '90

I WAS ALONE IN CINDY'S ROOM A LONG TIME BEFORE SHE CAME UPSTAIRS. THE SKY HAD TURNED WHITE AND SO MANY BIRDS HAD SHOT THEIR NOTES OUT THEN STOPPED AND THE SOUND OF THE WORLD WAS BLANK. THE DOOR OPENED.

"HI" SHE SAID. "HI" I SAID. BIG DEAL IF HER BROTHER THINKS I'M AN UPTIGHT PRUDE FOR LEAVING IN THE MIDDLE OF HIM TRYING THINGS. ANYWAY HE'S TOO OLD. FROM NOW ON IF CINDY WANTS TO SPEND THE NIGHT LET'S DO IT AT MY HOUSE. HE WHISPERED "YOU BITCH" TO ME. SCREW HIM. I GUESS CINDY HAD A BETTER TIME WITH HIS FRIEND AGNER CONSIDERING HOW LONG SHE WAS GONE.

SHE HAD TWO CIGARETTES. "WANT ONE?" I SAID NO. SHE CLIMBED ON THE BED TO SMOKE IT BY THE WINDOW BLOWING HER DRAGS OUT WITH HER MOUTH PRESSED AGAINST THE SCREEN. "AGNER'S DROPPING OUT." SHE SAID. "HE'S GONNA JOIN THE ARMY." IN THE WALLS I HEAR WATER START GOING THROUGH THE PIPES AND THE SOUND OF PANS DOWNSTAIRS. "HE WANTS ME TO BE TRUE TO HIM."

HER THUMB HOOKED UP A SILVER CHAIN AROUND HER NECK. "HE GAVE IT TO ME" AGNER'S SAINT CHRISTOPHER. SHE SWUNG IT AND SMILED. BEFORE THAT, CINDY ALWAYS SEEMED MY SAME AGE. NOW I SAW HOW MANY SPACES SHE HAD SKIPPED. I GUESS WHEN YOU ALREADY LOOK 17, YOU CAN. I GUESS THERE'S NO RULE SAYING 14 EVER HAS TO COUNT.

THE MOVIE
BY LYNDA WRONGHEADED BARRY © 1990
I SAW DOUG. IT WAS SO WEIRD. LIKE THE WORLD OF WHAT HAPPENED WITH US LAST WINTER NEVER EVEN EXISTED. HE WAS SO NICE AND TALKED TO ME SO NORMALLY I HAD TO FORCE MY BRAIN TO KEEP REMEMBERING.
HEY.

IT WAS AT THE A+W. MARLYS WAS IN LINE AND I WAS WAITING BY THE PICNIC TABLES AND WHEN HE FIRST CAME UP, I FELT LIKE I WENT INSIDE MY OWN STOMACH AND STARTED SCREAMING. "HI." HE SAID. "HI" I SAID BACK. AND HE WAS TALKING AND ACTING LIKE HE NEVER BROKE UP WITH ME AND ALL THE SADNESS WAS ONLY MY IMAGINATION.

AND THE WEIRDEST THING OF ALL WAS HOW I FELT SO HAPPY WHEN HE TOLD ME HOW HE ALWAYS WAS THINKING OF ME WHEN HE WAS WITH CINDY OR OTHER GIRLS OR WHOEVER. BECAUSE HE REALLY SOUNDED FOR REAL AND SINCERE. HE SAID HE WAS GOING THROUGH CHANGES AND THAT HE JUST REALIZED THAT I WAS DEEP AND HOW HE TREATED ME SO SHALLOW.

HERE.
HEY., HERE'S YOUR THING
HEY.

I DIDN'T KNOW WHAT TO DO BECAUSE TRULY I NEVER LOVED A GUY AS MUCH AS DOUG WHO WAS PERFECT IN EVERY-WAY EXCEPT FOR HIS COLD BLOODEDNESS TO ME. THEN I STARTED THINKING: IS THIS THE HAPPY ENDING? IS THIS THE INCREDIBLE ENDING TO THE MOVIE OF ME AND DOUG WHERE WE GET BACK TOGETHER?

YOU GOING?
YEAH.
CAN I WALK YOU?
UH...

A MESSAGE

BY LYNDA BLACK MAGIC WOMAN BARRY © 1990

DEAR BRENDA, SORRY I KEEP WRITING SO MUCH BUT I NEED YOUR ADVICE BEFORE I GO ON A FREAK OUT! REMEMBER THAT GUY DOUG WHO BROKE UP WITH ME AT CHRISTMAS? WELL GUESS WHAT, HE WANTS TO GET BACK WITH ME. HE TOLD ME HE HAS GONE THROUGH CHANGES

AND ALSO HE IS NOW 100% INTO JESUS CHRIST. IT'S CALLED "A JESUS FREAK." DO YOU KNOW ABOUT THEM? WHAT HAPPENED WAS HE TOOK ORANGE SUNSHINE LSD AT A CREEDENCE CONCERT AND WAS MAKING OUT WITH A GIRL JESUS FREAK. THIS WAS WHEN HE TOOK DRUGS AND ONLY USED GIRLS. HE SAID IT WAS A BUMMER TRIP TO MAKE OUT ON ACID AND HE WAS FREAKING OUT AND THOUGHT HE MIGHT THROW UP BUT HE DIDN'T WANT

TO TELL HER BECAUSE IF YOU SAY IT, IT HAPPENS. THEN HE SAID HER HEAD TURNED INTO HIS MOM AND HE HAD TO QUIT MAKING OUT AND THEN THE GIRL SAID "JESUS LOVES YOU" AND HER HEAD TURNED INTO JESUS BUT WITH NO BEARD AND RAYS CAME OUT OF THE MOUTH SAYING SOMETHING LIKE QUIT SCREWING YOUR LIFE UP. DOUG SAID IT WAS A MESSAGE.

THEN HE SAID THE GIRL TOLD HIM: TO ASK JESUS INTO HIS HEART, AND ALSO THAT SHE HAD A BOYFRIEND SO THERE WAS NO WAY FOR HER AND DOUG. SHE TOLD HIM SHE WAS SURE THERE WAS A GIRL WHO REALLY LOVED HIM AND THAT'S WHEN HE THOUGHT "OH YEAH. MAYBONNE." SO NOW HE WANTS TO GET BACK WITH ME ONLY I HAVE TO GET JESUS IN MY HEART FIRST. I DON'T KNOW WHAT TO DO. YOU KNOW HOW WEIRD I'VE BEEN FEELING ABOUT GOD. PLEASE WRITE ME WITH YOUR ADVICE!!!!
Love, Maybonne

WELCOME

BY LYNDA BARRY © 1990

WHAT DOES TAKING JESUS INTO YOUR HEART EVEN MEAN? DOUG WANTS ME BACK BUT HE SAYS HE CAN'T LOVE ME IF I DON'T HAVE JESUS. I TOLD HIM THAT'S WEIRD BECAUSE I HEARD THE BIG THING OF CHRISTIANS IS THEY ARE SUPPOSED TO LOVE EVERYBODY.

HE SAID SURE HE WOULD LOVE ME, BUT NO WAY COULD HE RELATE TO ME. THEN HE SAID: COULD I COME TO HIS ONE WAY YOUTH GROUP MEETING AND HE POINTED HIS FINGER UP WHEN HE SAID "ONE WAY." THAT'S THE RULE OF BEING IN ONE WAY. IF YOU SAY IT, YOU HAVE TO POINT YOUR FINGER UP.

WE WERE SITTING IN THE A+W PARKING LOT. EVERYTIME PEOPLE PASSED US DOUG SAID "HOWDY. JESUS LOVES YOU." HE WAS SMILING. HE TOLD ME HE WAS BLISSED OUT. THEN A GIRL NAMED THERESA WHO WAS IN HIS YOUTH GROUP CAME UP. "ONE WAY" SHE SAID. "ONE WAY" HE SAID. THEN THEY STARTED HUGGING FOR A REALLY LONG TIME WITH THEIR EYES CLOSED. I GOT JEALOUS. I SAID I WOULD GO TO ONE WAY.

DOUG SAYS WHEN JESUS COMES INTO YOUR HEART YOU START CRYING AND RAYS OF LIGHT COME ALL AROUND YOU. DOUG SAYS COMPARED TO JESUS, ACID IS NOTHING. THE MEETING IS TOMORROW. HE ALREADY TOLD THEM I WAS COMING. THEY'RE DOING A SPECIAL PRAYER DEAL JUST FOR ME.

READY READY
BY LYNDA "Listen to BONGO JOE" BARRY © 1990
DEAR BRENDA, WHAT IT IS. DO YOU KNOW JESUS? THAT'S THE QUESTION PEOPLE KEEP ASKING ME. I WENT TO DOUG'S CHRISTIAN ONE WAY YOUTH GROUP MEETING TO GET JESUS IN MY HEART BUT I MIGHT HAVE GOT THE INSTRUCTIONS WRONG.
I ACCEPT YOU AS MY PERSONAL SAVIOR.

IT WAS EMBARRASSING BECAUSE THEY DID A SPECIAL PRAYER DEAL JUST FOR ME. THEN THIS GIRL THERESA SAID PROBABLY I WASN'T READY YET BECAUSE I WAS STILL HOLDING ON TO SIN. ALSO THAT I SECRETLY DIDN'T WANT JESUS IN MY HEART. YOU CAN'T BELIEVE HOW EMBARRASSING IT WAS THAT SHE SAID THAT.

PLEASE COME INTO MY HEART.

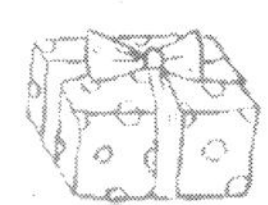

SHE LIKES DOUG AND IS JEALOUS OF ME SO NOW SHE IS GOING AROUND TELLING PEOPLE THINGS LIKE THE DEVIL IS HOLDING A PART OF MY HEART. SHE SHOULD TALK! WHAT A HYPOCRITE TO ACT LIKE SHE'S SO INTO JESUS WHEN THE REALITY IS SHE'S MORE INTO DOUG. DOUG SAYS DON'T LET HER FREAK ME OUT BECAUSE I'M ABOUT TO GO ON AN AMAZING JOURNEY.

DOES THIS SEEM WEIRD TO YOU THOUGH? HOW CHRISTIANS SAY THEY LOVE EVERYBODY BUT ALL I COULD HEAR WAS THEM PUTTING DOWN ALL THE PEOPLE NOT IN ONE WAY. ALSO THEY THINK THE DEVIL IS A REAL GUY NOT A CONCEPT. I'M GOING TO KEEP GOING THOUGH BECAUSE IF I GO TO TEN MEETINGS I CAN GO ON THE CAMP OUT RETREAT WHICH EVERYONE SAYS IS A BLAST. WRITE ME. LOVE,

Maybonne

MAYBE I'M NOT SAYING IT RIGHT.

SAVED

BY LYNDA "WHO STOLE MY BIKE?" BARRY © 1990

OUR FATHER WHO ART IN HEAVEN YOU KNOW I'VE BEEN GOING TO ONE WAY MEETINGS AND ASKING JESUS INTO MY HEART. YOU KNOW I TRIED SINCERELY 5 TIMES BUT THEY WERE ALL DUDS. OK. THEN I ADMIT I FAKED IT. I LEARNED HOW TO ACT IT THEN I FAKED IT.

I HAD TO. THAT GIRL THERESA WAS GETTING ON MY NERVES SAYING I WAS DIGGING ON THE DEVIL WHICH I AM NOT! SHE'S AFTER DOUG WHO SAYS I'M HIS FIRST PICK FOR A GIRLFRIEND BUT ONLY IF I HAVE JESUS SO YOU SEE MY PROBLEM. THERESA WAS TRYING TO POISON HIS MIND AGAINST ME! DEAR GOD I AM HEARTILY SORRY NOT ONLY BECAUSE I LIED BUT ALSO BECAUSE I'M SCREWED.

I USED TO GIVE MY OPINIONS AT THE MEETINGS ON THEIR CRITICAL CONCEPTS LIKE THE GROUP IRON BUTTERFLY IS A SYMBOL OF THE DEVIL. THEN THEY ACTED LIKE "OH. YOU CAN'T UNDERSTAND IT UNTIL YOU GET JESUS." NOW I HAVE TO ACT LIKE I UNDERSTAND IT BECAUSE OTHERWISE I WILL BE BUSTED. AND LOSE DOUG, WHO I LOVE, FOREVER. THE END.

ARE YOU RIDING ON ANOTHER BUMMER AGAIN?
KIND OF.
IT'S THAT DOUG GUY.
KIND OF.

LAST NIGHT THEY SAID <u>NO LISTENING TO THE SONG HOUSE OF THE RISING SUN</u>. MY FAVORITE SONG. I JUST SAT THERE. THEY SAID <u>NO BLACK LIGHT POSTERS IN ANYONE'S LIFE</u>. I DIDN'T SAY ANYTHING. IN THE CHURCH PARKING LOT SOME <u>ONE WAY</u> PEOPLE SAID <u>JEWS</u>, <u>NIGGERS</u>, <u>QUEERS</u> AND MORE WORDS AND I JUST STOOD THERE. DOUG HAD HIS ARM AROUND ME. DEAR GOD WHICH IS MY WORST SIN?

YOU CAN SAY YOUR TROUBLES TO ME IF YOU WANT.

THANKS BUT IT'S HARD TO EXPLAIN.

THAT'S OK.

TURNS OUT

BY LYNDA BARRY WITH SCOTT C. NEWMAN © 1990

DEAR BRENDA. PEACE SISTER. WELL I GUESS THE THING I WAS DOING WITH JESUS IS ALL OVER. TURNS OUT THE LEADER OF ONE WAY WAS TRYING TO GET IT ON WITH SOME OF THE ONE WAY GIRLS AND ALSO SMOKED POT IN A WATER PIPE.

IT ALL CAME DOWN SATURDAY AT THE YOUTH CENTER. THERE'S PEOPLE SAYING I WAS THE NARC BUT I WASN'T. ALSO DOUG WAS BUSTED WITH POT AND HE WAS GOING AROUND ACTING LIKE THE HUGEST CHRISTIAN OF ALL! FROM THE PEOPLE I MET IN ONE WAY I FEEL SORRY FOR JESUS GETTING STUCK WITH THEM FOR WORSHIPPERS. WHAT A RIP.

ME AND DOUG ARE NOT TOGETHER. ALL DURING ONE WAY HE THOUGHT I WAS NOT PURE ENOUGH FOR HIM. BEFORE I CARED BUT NOW I DON'T. I'M BACHE-LORETTE #1 NOW. THERE'S A GUY AT THE A+W WHO'S SEMI-CUTE. HEY GUESS WHAT? REMEMBER MRS. BROGAN FROM 5th GRADE? MARLYS HAD A DREAM HER HEAD WAS IMPLANTED ON OUR TV.

SHE TOLD ME MRS. BROGAN'S HEAD WAS THE ANTENNA AND YOU TWISTED IT AROUND TO GET BETTER CHANNELS. TALK ABOUT NATURALLY STONED! SHE WAS TRIPPING WAY OUT TO GET THAT IDEA! HEY LISTEN TO ME YOU DOG, YOU BETTER WRITE ME!!! CAN YOU BELIEVE IT'S ALMOST SCHOOL AGAIN? PRAY FOR ME TO GET DECENT TEACHERS! POWER TO THE PEOPLE RIGHT ON TO ALL PEOPLE

Love, Maybonne

Spazzy right on hand. Look How I can't even draw!

THE LAST MINUTE

by LYNDA BARRY 1990

IT WAS THE LAST NIGHTS OF SUMMER AND ALL OF US WENT INTO THIS THING OF COMING ONTO THE PLAYFIELD UP AT SELMER AFTER DINNER. SOMETIMES THE SHRIMPS WERE PLAYING KICK BALL BUT MOSTLY EVERYONE HUNG OUT ON THE STEPS.

THERE WAS SMOKING AND DARE-YOUS TO: CLIMB THE SCHOOL, TELL EMBARRASSING DETAILS OF YOUR LIFE, CHUG A WHOLE BOTTLE OF TAB. IN THE DARK SOMETIMES SOMEBODY AND SOMEBODY ELSE WOULD GO FOR A LAST MAKE-OUT IN THE BUSHES, OR TELL A STORY YOU NEVER HEARD BEFORE ABOUT A THING SO SAD. WE HUNG OUT ON THE STEPS GETTING A NIGHT FEELING.

THEN YOU WOULD HEAR THE MOMS START CALLING FOR THE SHRIMPS AND THEN THE SHRIMPS COME YELLING FOR YOU. HOW YOU WERE GOING TO GET IT IF YOU DIDN'T COME HOME. ONE MORE CIGARETTE. ONE MORE HOPE THAT AT THE LAST MINUTE YOU COULD ALSO GET A MAKE OUT. BIG DEAL IF YOU GOT IN TROUBLE BECAUSE THE FEELING IS SO WORTH IT.

MINE WAS WITH TOM BY THE FENCE. I COULD HEAR THE VOICE OF MY SISTER COMING CLOSER. OH THE BRACES OF TOM ON MY LIPS, HIM PUSHING UP AGAINST ME. THAT THING OF PLEASE GOD PUSH THE BUTTON ON TIME, LET ME NEVER HAVE TO GO BACK HOME.

THE FIRST DAY

BY LYNDA "LOOKIN AT YOU" BARRY © 1991

PLEASE LET THIS YEAR'S SCHOOL BE GOOD. LET ME GET DECENT TEACHERS, HAVE PEOPLE I LIKE TO SIT WITH AT LUNCH AND KEEP ME AWAY FROM DOUG.

LET ME DO GOOD AT ALL MY SUBJECTS, KEEP MY HAIR, CLOTHES, AND BODY FROM LOOKING WARPED, AND MAKE IT SO PEOPLE DON'T THINK I'M WEIRD. OR IF THEY ARE GOING TO THINK I'M WEIRD LET IT BE FOR A GOOD REASON WHERE IN THE END, I TURN OUT TO BE RIGHT AND THEN THEY FEEL WEIRD BUT THEN I GO "IT'S OK, DON'T FEEL WEIRD." BUT I MEAN IT.

LET PREJUDICE, POLLUTION, WAR, AND THE POPULATION EXPLOSION BE TOPICS NOT JUST FOR REPORTS BUT ALSO FOR REAL ACTION. ON MY HONOR I WILL DO MY BEST TO DO MY DUTY TO GOD AND MY COUNTRY BUT IT MIGHT NOT BE THE SAME GOD AS THE GOD OF THE CHURCH AND I MIGHT NOT BE DIGGING ON THE MESSAGE OF THE PRESIDENT BECAUSE THE WINDMILLS OF HIS MIND ARE CRACKED ON A LOT OF SUBJECTS CONCERNING PEOPLE.

MAYBONNE! WAIT!
WAIT!

AND IF YOU WANT TO SEND ME A GREAT BOYFRIEND WHO IS NICE I THINK I COULD STAND IT THIS YEAR. AND I PROMISE TO TRY TO DO BETTER AND NOT MESS UP SO BAD. TRULY I ALSO THANK YOU FOR LAST YEAR. IT WAS INCREDIBLE EVEN THOUGH PARTS DID MAKE ME ABOUT BARF FROM SAD-NESS, I STILL SAY RIGHT ON! I CAN'T BELIEVE IT FINALLY IS THE FIRST DAY OF SCHOOL!

HOPE IT GOES GOOD TODAY!

Home Economics
maybelline
Long Longer Longest
one is the lonliest number
1 cup
Drama
Algebra
Diary
Libra
Cutex
Taurus
Born Free
In the year 2525
Leo
I'm thinking bout the love that you laid on my table
Beautiful People don't Criticize
Cancer
Meet the Swinger
Maybonne + ???
art
Spirit in the sky
Fools said I you do not know
MILK BONE
BAGS
If you're going to San